Praise for *Los*

Many of us are devoted to the pets as well as the wild
creatures that share the world with us. Their deaths
can be wrenching, yet the culture we live in often
trivializes our grief. With empathy and tenderness, Jeffrey
Moussaieff Masson writes of the innate dignity of other
animals and the strength and beauty of our mutual bond
- illuminating our right to love them, and mourn their
leaving, as deeply as we want.

—PULITZER FINALIST LYDIA MILLET, AUTHOR OF *FIGHT
NO MORE, OMNIVORES,* AND *A CHILDREN'S BIBLE*

A thoughtful examination of a heartbreaking thing that
happens to many of us, the death of a beloved pet, *Lost
Companions* is a beautiful book about a largely ignored
subject, and will help many people.

—ELIZABETH MARSHALL THOMAS, *NEW YORK TIMES*
BESTSELLING AUTHOR OF *THE HIDDEN LIVES OF DOGS*

Losing a pet or other animal friend can be incredibly
traumatic. This touching book is all about the bonds
between humans and other species, and why we grieve
their loss as much as we do.

—FRANS DE WAAL, *NEW YORK TIMES* BESTSELLING
AUTHOR OF *MAMA'S LAST HUG: ANIMAL EMOTIONS AND
WHAT THEY TELL US ABOUT OURSELVES*

Also by Jeffrey Moussaieff Masson

Lost Companions

Reflections on the
Death of Pets

Jeffrey Moussaieff Masson

murdoch books
Sydney | London

First published in the United States in 2020 by St. Martin's Press,
an imprint of St. Martin's Publishing Group

Published in 2020 by Murdoch Books, an imprint of Allen & Unwin '

Murdoch Books Australia
83 Alexander Street, Crows Nest NSW 2065
Phone: +61 (0)2 8425 0100
murdochbooks.com.au
info@murdochbooks.com.au

Murdoch Books UK
Ormond House, 26–27 Boswell Street, London WC1N 3JZ
Phone: +44 (0) 20 8785 5995
murdochbooks.co.uk
info@murdochbooks.co.uk

A catalogue record for this
book is available from the
National Library of Australia

A catalogue record for this book is available from the British Library

ISBN 978 1 92235 115 9 Australia
ISBN 978 1 91166 801 5 UK

Design by Donna Sinisgalli Noetzel
Cover photography by iStock_ chendongshan

Printed and bound in Australia by Griffin Press
10 9 8 7 6 5 4 3 2 1

The paper in this book is FSC® certified.
FSC® promotes environmentally responsible,
socially beneficial and economically viable
management of the world's forests.

For Ilan

Contents

Acknowledgments

This book is dedicated to my son Ilan because in addition to all the ways my life has been immeasurably enriched by the existence of Ilan and my other son, Manu, I owe him a deep debt of gratitude for being with Benjy for two years in Berlin and giving him the love he deserved while he himself got the special love that Benjy is famous for. I would fully expect the same from our younger son, Manu, who has lived with Benjy almost his entire life. I credit his extraordinary gentleness and kindness, in part at least, to having always lived with animals.

I want to thank my old friend Andy Ross (whom I knew in the days when he was the owner of the legendary Cody's Books on Telegraph Avenue in Berkeley), now my literary agent. He is the only agent I have ever known who will answer an email in seconds! He has another sterling quality: as my good friend Daniel Ellsberg said to me recently after the three of us got together for coffee, and after Andy had left: "Jeffrey, you never told me Andy was so entertaining!"

I am grateful to my wife, Leila, for reading the book and making her usual penetrating observations. She has been the light of my life for the last twenty-five years. I owe her everything.

I also want to acknowledge my much-loved daughter, Simone, who lived with many dogs and cats as she was growing up (and nearly became a vet as a result). Watching her feel such wonderful and important emotions for animals certainly played a major role in inspiring me to write about animal emotions.

Clare Wadsworth, a family friend, and editor who lives in the South of France with a pack of dogs, read over my manuscript, made many useful suggestions, but most importantly, she gave me the stimulus to continue when I thought I simply could not continue.

Jenny Miller has read and provided commentary on just about every book I have ever written, and this one was no exception. We share a love of dogs and a dislike of psychiatry, and her comments are always wise and on target. I am very grateful for all the help she has given me over the years.

So many people gave me great stories about their pets, that I could not possibly thank them all. Most of them are identified in the book along with their stories, and I am delighted that so many people were willing to share their stories, their grief, and their love for many different animals. I have also learned a great deal from the many wonderful books written about dogs, cats, and other animals. They continue to be written in ever greater numbers, a testimony to the fact that we are just beginning to discover the wonder of "others." Just today I finished the magnificent book by Sigrid Nunez, *The Friend: A Novel,* which won the 2018 National Book Award, about the deep friendship (indeed, love) between a woman and a dog, which is just brimming with ideas that might not have been possible to contemplate just a few years ago. I urge the book on all animal lovers.

Those of us who love dogs, cats, and birds understand that other people feel just as strongly for countless other animals who are not usually thought of as pets. I think of my friends David Brooks and Teya Pribac who feel the same love for their rescued sheep who live with them in idyllic surroundings in the Blue Mountains near Sydney. Teya has just written a brilliant Ph.D. thesis that helped to clarify for me that animals feel grief every bit as much as humans do.

As I was writing this book, I would have lunch once a week with the amazing Brian Sherman (who, with his equally amazing daughter, Ondine, founded the animal-rights organization Voiceless), and always present was Miracle, the dog who would not leave Brian's side for a minute, even more so now that Miracle knows that not all is well with Brian, which just makes her more determined to stick close to her best friend. It was an inspiration to observe, and helped me think about the deeper themes of this book.

Acknowledgments

My most important acknowledgment is for the love I have received during my life from countless dogs and cats, and birds, and even rats, chickens, and bunny rabbits, which has enriched my life beyond my ability to entirely articulate it.

Finally, I must say something about the wonderful staff at St. Martin's Press, beginning with the very patient, very talented Daniela Rapp, who I was fortunate enough to have as my editor. She pushed me to expand the contents of this book in ways I had not initially planned, but I can see now that those additions greatly added to the book. Thank you, Daniela, for bringing in a larger vision of what this book could be. She was assisted by David Stanford Burr, Mattew Carrera, Alyssa Gammello, Cassidy Graham, Brant Janeway, Erica Martirano, Donna Noetzel, Ervin Serrano, and Vincent Stanley.

Because I live in Australia, and because we have just had a catastrophic string of fires that have led to the death of over a billion animals (hard as that is to conceive), I felt I should say something about how that makes not just me but most Australians feel. In a word: terrible.

The popular phrase goes: the death of a single person is a tragedy, but a million is a statistic. I don't believe this. I think it is one of the few characteristics of humans that may surpass the ability of animals: we can imagine and react to the death of animals we do not know. It is not an abstraction. It is real. For many people, seeing a photo of a single koala sitting in deep grief and suffering was not something they could shrug off. It touched a nerve in millions of Australians. It stood for the one billion who had been killed. Each one was an individual, with a biography, a life story, with friends, family, possibly children. We can easily and uncomfortably imagine the panic and distress when the fires came and there was nowhere safe to run. Some humans died too, but most of us had a means of escape. Those billion did not. Think of it: one billion, it is such an unthinkable figure, but it means a terrible and painful death — sometimes quick, but at other times slow and drawn out, with nobody there to offer comfort or explanation.

In this book, I wonder whether dogs and other animals who live with us understand death, know when it is coming, and are frightened when it arrives. My conclusion is that they do. I quote an anonymous veterinarian who begged people who bring their animals to him for euthanasia, not to leave at the last moment, because the animal will frantically scan the room, looking for the person they know and are familiar with. For comfort. So, as hard as it may be for some to stay and be there in the final moment of their beloved animal's life, please do so, he pleads. I agree with him. It's essential for the sake of the animal to stay, if you can, which is why it's so unbearable to imagine hundreds of millions of animals enduring their final moments with nobody there to witness or bring them solace. We don't usually stop to think of the suffering of wild animals, but this destruction has hopefully reminded us of how our lives impact theirs, and how interconnected our worlds are

I know that when many people saw the photo of the young koala looking so defeated, they had to weep. But we cannot weep a billion times. We cannot feel the sadness a billion times, or we could not continue to live. But we can keep it in our mind, we can try to understand it, and we can feel it in our hearts. It is, ultimately, what makes us want to do something to rescue our planet and the billions of other animals and people on it before it is too late, and they too succumb the way the Australian animals have.

It is a wake-up call, and it speaks well of our species that we can be awakened, and we can care about the fate of animals we do not know personally. Some of us care very deeply, so much so that sometimes it feels as if we cannot continue our daily life with such raw feelings pressing in on us. We would prefer to go to bed and wake up from what was just a nightmare. Alas, we cannot do this. But at least we can recognise the kinship — how all those animals are just as dependent on our earth as we are, and that we are all in this together. We must struggle together to make a safer world for us, human animals, and for all other non-human animals on our endangered planet.

—JEFFREY MOUSSAIEFF MASSON, PH.D., MARCH 2020
TAMARAMA, NSW, AUSTRALIA

My Encounter with the Angel of Death

The dog of your boyhood teaches you a great deal
about friendship, and love, and death: Old Skip
was my brother. They had buried him under our
elm tree, they said—yet this wasn't totally true.
For he really lay buried in my heart.

—WILLIE MORRIS, *MY DOG SKIP*

I have just finished reading the fine book by Frans de
Waal, *Mama's Last Hug: Animal Emotions and What They
Teach Us about Ourselves*. The title of the book comes from
an extraordinary moment in the relation between two different species: "Mama" as she was called by the humans
who observed her at Burgers Zoo at Arnhem in the Nether-
lands, was the matriarch chimpanzee in a large colony. She
had become close, over many years, with the distinguished
Dutch zoologist Jan van Hoof (emeritus professor of be-
havioral biology at Utrecht University and cofounder of
the Burgers colony). A month before she turned fifty-nine,
she lay dying. Her friend, the zoologist, was about to turn
eighty. They had known each other for more than forty
years but he had not seen her for a long time. When Jan

heard she was dying, he came to say good-bye. This was in 2016, and somebody who was there took a cell phone video of what transpired. It is astonishing. The chimps actually live on a forested island in the zoo, the largest such structure in the world (to me this is still a form of captivity, but that is a discussion for another day). Mama was confined to a cage since her attendants had to attempt to feed her. She was lying on a straw mat, and would not move or eat or drink. What happened next, caught on video and seen more than ten million times, is heartrending.*

Her carers are attempting to feed her with a spoon, but she refuses both food and drink. She is listless, and hardly responsive. She looks very close to death. But Jan comes in and begins to stroke her. She slowly rouses herself, and then looks up. She looks somewhat bewildered as if not understanding who is there. But then it appears she recognizes him, and she suddenly gives a shriek of delight. He pats her saying over and over, "yes, yes, it is me," and she reaches out to him with a giant and unmistakable smile on her face, and reaches up to touch his face with her finger, very gently. He reassures her with gentle words of comfort. She combs his hair with her fingers. He strokes her face, and she touches his head over and over, as he says, "yes, Mama, yes." She pulls him closer until their

---

* You can see the video here: https://www.youtube.com/watch?v=INa -oOAexno.

faces are touching. They are both clearly moved far beyond words, and Jan goes silent as he continues to stroke
Mama's face. She then falls back into her fetal position.
She died a few weeks later. I defy anyone to watch this
encounter without being moved to tears.

But why? Why do we cry when we see this love across
the species barrier? I believe it is a deep and ancient long-
ing, to bond with a member of a different species. It is
something of a miracle that we have created the possibility
of doing this with great ease between two domesticated
species: cats and dogs. There are many people who also
achieve this with horses and with birds, and a few who
experience it with completely wild species. I will write
about all of these in this book. But what I am writing about
here is not just the fact that we have achieved this miracle,
and that we are both astonished and delighted by our suc-
cess, but that we are as reluctant to give it up, at the end,
as we are when the same circumstances force us to depart
from our loved humans. There is no greater challenge than
facing the death of a beloved intimate, whether it be your
mother or father, your child, your friend, your spouse, or
the animal you have come to love like any other member
of the family. What we see in the video of "Mama's Last
Hug," is that it can happen even with a wild animal, and
even one in captivity. Death seems to be the great leveler
here, and it does not matter who mourns whom, the grief
on both sides is tangible, and profound.

While immersed in writing this book, I had what Sigmund Freud called "a big dream"; that is, one freighted with significance. A woman with a bow and a quiver full of arrows suddenly appeared in front of me and my wife, Leila. I knew she was the Angel of Death. She offered me another life (A different life? This life, only longer?) if I would allow her to shoot me in the heart with an arrow. "It will hurt and there will be a lot of blood," she explained. But the outcome would be that I could continue to live for a long time. I agreed. When it would take place was unclear. Later, still in the dream, I went on a bike ride in the hills with my twenty-three-year-old son, Ilan. When my bike lost a wheel, Ilan went into a cave to have it fixed and suddenly the sky changed colors dramatically. I knew the moment had come and I had a feeling unlike any I have ever had in real life, a mixture of terror and excitement. But even as I felt it, I knew that I would never have this feeling again. I was both at peace and also terribly frightened, because I understood that what was about to happen would be painful in the extreme. The Angel of Death was once again in front of me. She nodded as if to say "the moment is here." She took a sharp arrow from her quiver, placed it on the string of her bow, drew the string back, and aimed at my heart. I steeled myself for the blow. *This is it,* I thought. *This is the most important moment of your life.* I was as frightened as I have ever been, but I was also intensely curious as to how it would play out.

Suddenly I woke up. My heart was beating fast. I was still caught up in the dream. What struck me as unique was not the bargain, but the feeling I had when the Angel of Death came for me the second time and the sky changed. That was like no feeling I have ever actually experienced in real life. It was a dream feeling that I cannot describe. I could remember the feeling, though it began to fade as the day progressed, but I am at a loss to put it into words or to compare it to anything else I have ever felt. What moved me most forcibly was when the sky suddenly changed, becoming very dark, and then light again. It was as if something important was about to happen to the world, and then I knew it was just me. There was no change in the world, only in my own fate. When the angel appeared in front of me for the final time, I was frightened, but also in a kind of ecstasy. *Death is not the end,* I thought, without actually thinking it in so many words. I was intensely curious and deeply disappointed when I suddenly awoke— nobody woke me, I just woke up, perhaps out of fear of the coming arrow—that now I would never know what might have happened, even if it was only a dream. Would the blow hurt? But I would survive and know that now I would live for another twenty or thirty years?

It is not insignificant that I dreamed this while writing a book about death, and in particular the approaching death of our beloved dog Benjy, who is now living with Ilan in Berlin and is nearing his fourteenth birthday.

I would love to make a bargain with the Angel of Death for Benjy—and while she is there, why not for me as well, as I begin to see the outlines of eighty in front of me? What could be more human than to wish for more life just as ours is coming to a close? This is also a universal desire that applies not just to ourselves, but to the animals in our lives. We wish they could live longer, even as long as we live.

We cannot look into the eyes of every other animal species on the planet (think of insects and reptiles), and see ourselves echoed. We cannot read what is happening inside every animal whose eyes we meet. I am of course not saying that the animals whose eyes tell us nothing are feeling nothing, simply that we are not attuned to each other. But we are attuned to certain animals. Primarily to dogs and cats, but there are also wild animals whose eyes betray deep feeling that we have little problem in reading.

The fear of anthropomorphizing, that is, attributing to animals thoughts and sentiments that belong strictly to humans, has been replaced by what some scientists are calling anthropodenial, that is, the all too common refusal to recognize our similarity to other animals, especially when it comes to feelings and emotions. It could well be, as I will describe later in the book, that some animals actually feel some emotions more deeply than we do (love in dogs, contentment in cats, mourning in elephants) but this is a field of inquiry that has not yet been sufficiently explored.

And at no time is there any greater understanding between living creatures than at the point of death. Suddenly we understand something, and it would appear they do, too. What that something is, is hard to put into words. It is known, felt, acknowledged, understood, but it does not easily lend itself to description, or even explanation. Anyone who has been present at the death of their dog knows what I am speaking about. Astonishingly, it can also happen with a far more "alien" species—in this case I am thinking of a whale. There was an article on the BBC News by Andreas Illmer about a travel blogger from the United States, Liz Carlson who, while hiking with a friend, came across 145 whales beached and dying on a remote New Zealand beach.[*]

"It was one of these jaw-dropping moments," she told the BBC. "We came to the beach around sunset and spotted something in the shallows.

"When we realized it was whales, we dropped everything and ran into the surf."

She'd seen whales in the wild before, she said, but "nothing can prepare you for this, it was just horrific. The futility was the worst. They are crying out to each other and are talking and clicking, and there's no way to help them."

---

[*] Illmer, Andreas. "New Zealand Whale Stranding: 'I Will Never Forget Their Cries'." *BBC News,* BBC, November 27, 2018, www.bbc.com/news/world -asia-46354618.

Her friend, Julian Ripoll, set off for help.

She was alone, in despair, "I'll never forget their cries, the way they watched me as I sat with them in the water, how they desperately tried to swim, but their weight only dug them deeper into the sands," she wrote on Instagram.

"My heart completely broke."

As does ours, the readers. What strikes me most is that the whales looked to her for help, much as our dogs do in their dying moments. "Is there nothing you can do?" is the message I get, as did she, which is why she said her heart was breaking because the only answer is no, there is nothing I can do except witness your end.

This is a book about witnessing the end. Are we perhaps the angels of death? Alas, we have no power to bargain on behalf of our loved ones. But we are not helpless. We can do more than simply witness the death of our beloved animals. We can help them in their last moments and that help makes an enormous difference to them (and probably to us as well). In this book I will look at just how this happens, and what I and others have found most helpful that we can do for our animals as they approach the end. Knowing that we are literally "there" makes an enormous difference to them. This is the least we owe them. It is heartbreaking, but everyone I have spoken to who has been there at the very end is glad, for their own sake, and for the sake of their loved companion, that they were there and fully present.

INTRODUCTION

∞

Grieving for an Animal
Is What Makes Us Human Animals

Not the least hard thing to bear when they go from
us, these quiet friends, is that they carry away
with them so many years of our own lives.

—JOHN GALSWORTHY

It is a disorienting and odd feeling to have loved a dog or
cat or another animal for so long, and suddenly realize
that the end is approaching. This is such a complex feeling
that we endure: the knowledge that a period in our life has
come to an end; that the animal we have so loved and who
has been such an important part of our everyday life, is
about to leave us; that soon all we will have left are memories; that we are helpless to prevent what always strikes
us as a death too soon. It is different than the impending
death of a human companion—we can talk to them, and
reminisce, and discuss what is happening. But when a dog
feels the end approaching, and I am convinced they do,

1

they turn their eyes to us in a different kind of way. We cannot entirely understand what they are asking, but it breaks our hearts anyway.

Recently, I began to reflect about Benjy's prospective death. Benjy is a thirteen-year-old yellow Labrador. He has lived with me, my wife Leila, and our two boys, Ilan and Manu, for the last eleven years. His life expectancy is between ten and twelve, so the time is coming when he will die. I find that idea unbearable. Suppose things get so bad that I have to call the vet and have him come and give an injection as I hold Benjy in my arms, and I have to watch as the life leaves him? In my mind I see him give me a look of profound incomprehension, and then lick me. Why do I imagine it happening like this? Because I have heard it from so many people—friends, strangers, and readers of my books on the emotional lives of animals. Nothing brings home to us the depth of our relations to cats and dogs, and other animals who share our lives, like their deaths. Their lives are so much shorter than humans'. We know death is coming, and no matter how much we steel ourselves to the inevitable, it comes as a shock. I am trying to understand why this should be. Maybe because these animals look to us for help, and when they are dying, they want us to stop it from happening. And that is just what we want to do but cannot. We feel suddenly helpless, and are confronted with mortality in general, writ large in these animals who have become family, but in some sense even more than family—maybe part of ourselves.

Whenever I mentioned to friends that I was thinking of writing a book on this topic, invariably everyone had a story. Even my optometrist friend in Auckland, Grant Watters, said to me, "I can't think of anything worse than my dog dying." As he pointed out, their IQ might not be the highest, but their EQ, their emotional intelligence, is in the stratosphere! I completely agree.

In this book I want to explore these themes, by reflecting about the deaths of companion animals, using as sources the many letters I receive, conversations with friends who have lost their animals, and with veterinarians who have put animals down for their human companions—avoiding the politically loaded term *owners*. My primary focus will be on dogs and cats, but I will range further and also look at other animals with whom we share our lives. I would suggest there has been a change over the decades: once we were supposed to get over this quickly. Today mourning a lost animal is considered healthy and appropriate. In this book, I will look more closely at the psychology of loss.

It has been argued that dogs and cats do not have a sense of death. I am not sure this is true. Of course one could say it is merely conjecture, but so many of the accounts I have heard and read indicate that the dog or the cat (possibly less than dogs) actually looks to the human

in a unique way at the moment of death, as if recogniz-
ing that this is the final good-bye and aware of the depth
of the occasion. It is *not* like saying good-bye for the day,
and the dog, I believe, realizes this. Death could well be
as relevant to them as it is to us. This to me says that our
relations with other animals is far deeper than we have
usually been willing to recognize. The emotional bond is
nothing less than the one between parent and child. We
do not expect to lose a child and, when the animal dies,
the feeling is similar.

I have been thinking about the subject of this book
nearly my entire life, as have many people—and for the
same reason. Loss. I had a beloved cocker spaniel for
many years when I was very young. When I was ten, we
found Taffy dead in our backyard, long before she should
have died. My parents told me she had been poisoned by
a mean neighbor who did not like hearing our dog bark or
watching him race around our yard.

I was beside myself, as I am sure any child is, when
their "best friend" suddenly dies. I can still remember
the moment I saw Taffy's dead body, and how perplexed
I was and then how I suddenly burst into tears realizing
that Taffy would not come back with me that day or any
other day. Death may be hard to understand for a child,
but I understood perfectly that something had left my life
and would not return. I could not be consoled. I just felt
heartache and I think it would have been best for some-

one close to me to simply say they understood. Instead I was told what I knew were lies, namely that Taffy was waiting for me somewhere in the vast beyond and that we would be reunited. Also, that Taffy did not suffer, when I could see her purple tongue protruding from her mouth and to me, it looked like she died in agony, which I am sure is what happens when a dog is poisoned. It took me a long time to get over this first death and even now at seventy-nine years old, I can still remember the feelings I had then and the sense of loss that never entirely left me.

Is the grief we feel when a companion animal dies a popular topic? Indeed it is. Just recently there was a column in *The New York Times* by the author Jennifer Weiner: "What the President Doesn't Get About Dogs," in which she writes about how when her dog Wendell died, "it felt like the world had been knocked off its orbit." The "us" vs. "them" attitude that we have been accustomed to in terms of our relationship with animals is beginning to lose its hold. We see this even in popular culture, as the film *The Shape of Water* demonstrates: the river "monster" in the film is capable of far deeper love than the scientist intent on destroying him.

The more we know an animal personally, the more we are likely to accord them emotional and cognitive complexity. Any nonvegetarian (I address this topic more directly in chapter 12) is put immediately outside their comfort zone when looking into the eye of a pig or a cow.

It is too much like looking into the eye of your neighbor. To reach this point you don't need to do a whole lot of research, you just need to look. It may be mysterious, but it's not a mystery: these living beings are every bit as complex as we are, especially when we enter the realm of feelings.

I remember how outraged people were when General William Westmoreland said in the Oscar-winning 1974 Vietnam documentary *Hearts and Minds* "The Oriental doesn't put the same high price on life as does a Westerner. Life is plentiful. Life is cheap in the Orient." Could he have believed this or was it just convenient? After all, if you are responsible for the death of some three million people, it probably helps your conscience to think they did not mind dying. A lot has changed since the 1970s in our attitude toward both other ethnicities and other animals. The battle for the recognition of dogs and other animals as sentient, and thus fully capable of suffering as much or more than human animals may not have been completely won, but scientists are now far more inclined than they were some years ago to acknowledge sentience in animals we know (but not the ones we do not know!). Moreover, we also recognize that this battle is not entirely unrelated to the one for the recognition of equality among ethnicities. What would ever induce anyone to think that one race or ethnicity is superior to any other?

And so, if we accord these animals dignity in life,

we should obviously do the same in death. The death of any animal is an occasion for solemnity. I doubt that any reader has managed to avoid the sorrow that comes when saying good-bye to an animal they loved.

I have many such memories. One in particular has stuck with me. When I was a graduate student in India, many years ago, I had a strange incident with a dog. His mother was killed by a car in front of my house and when I heard the sound of the accident, I rushed out to find the mother dead and a small puppy, just a few weeks old, wailing in despair. I could not say what kind of dog he was—maybe just what Indians call a village dog. He looked like a kind of terrier, very small with white fur and black-tipped ears. I took him into my house, and so began a strange yearlong relationship between me and Puppy, as I called him. As might be expected, I became his mother, in fact his everything, and he would never leave my side.

He was not, however, a healthy dog. I was working on my Ph.D. in Sanskrit and, as the time came closer for me to return to Harvard, I was increasingly worried about what would happen to Puppy. I could not take him back to Cambridge, that was for sure. Finally, I found a family that agreed to take him. They lived in the country, far from the university.

I had the privilege of working with one of India's greatest traditional scholars, Pandit Srinivasa Shastri. He was a consummate Sanskrit scholar but spoke no English. So he and I communicated in classical Sanskrit, much to the amusement, or sometimes the astonishment, of bystanders. He was very orthodox, and his religion prohibited him from teaching a foreigner the finer points of the sacred language. However, we liked each other enormously, and he agreed to teach me on condition that I come to his office in the university before 6 AM when nobody would see me. Being an early riser, this suited me fine.

But he would not let me bring Puppy, as he shared some of the prejudices that many orthodox Hindus had (or have?) against dogs: they are considered unclean and should never be touched. The day arrived when I had to relinquish Puppy. With great sadness I watched as he was driven away, his eyes fixed on me from the back of the car in disbelief and obvious agony. He had never been separated from me like this before.

The next morning I went to visit my pandit at the assigned time. I was sad and I explained why. He was not terribly sympathetic; I could tell. *Kukurrasneha* he called it—love for a dog. It was not celebrated in the sacred texts, except, I later learned, in a wonderful story from the great Indian epic, the *Mahabharata,* which I will relate later in the book. After about half an hour we heard a noise at the door. We looked at each other in disbelief. Who could be there at this ungodly hour? And what did they want with us? Had my pandit been caught teaching an illicit student? I opened the door but nobody was there. Instead, in rushed a very excited Puppy! He made it clear that he was overjoyed that he had found me. Srinivasa was not, however. He shrieked and jumped up on the desk so as not to be defiled by the touch of Puppy, who looked determined, in his joy, to lick everything in sight.

But then Srinivasa must have suddenly realized that this small dog had somehow found his way to an empty university just a day after having been taken miles away. We heard later that a small dog had been observed to jump on the bus and gotten off at the university stop. Srinivasa's attitude changed completely: known for his eloquence and skill at extemporaneous rhyming, he looked compassionately at Puppy and made up a Sanskrit verse to the effect that we had been together in a previous life and karma insisted we stay together in this one.

I was so dumbfounded by the strange encounter that I did not know what to think. I could not even imagine how Puppy had found me. I took him home, with Srinivasa telling me in a most stern manner that I was never under any circumstances to abandon him again, even if it meant living the rest of my (his?) life in India. I was inclined to agree with his admonition. But it was a dilemma.

That evening I was discussing it with my best friend Robert Goldman, also a graduate student in Sanskrit and a dog lover like myself. As we sat there in the quiet dusk of a hot summer night in Poona, Puppy lay on my lap, gazing at me lovingly. He was so obviously relieved to have found me. I can only imagine how he had suffered, perhaps fearing that I had given him away? Suddenly he let out a huge sigh, his whole small body trembling from the effort, and he fixed his gaze on me with love—of that there can be no question. I was deeply moved. Then, his eyes still fixed on me with an odd look, he suddenly lay still. He had died.

It was not my first experience of the death of a beloved dog, but it was the one that got me thinking about the deaths of all animals to whom we become close. I want to understand the grief we feel under these circumstances, and to explore further that mysterious bond we share with the animals who enter our lives and become, without a shadow of a doubt, family.

I am sure all readers, or most of them, will agree with me that dogs are family. And yet, several friends who have lost children *and* dogs have written to me to express the profound difference. Yes, they acknowledge, losing a beloved dog is a terrible experience, not to be made light of, that can have a serious impact. But, they tell me, it is *nothing* like losing a child. I cannot dispute this, because I have never lost a child, and I know I would find it hard to even survive if I did. What they tell me feels right, but on the other hand I am not sure why one needs to engage in this comparison of suffering. What is important is to stress, especially for anyone from "outside"—that is to somebody who has lost neither—that it is a completely humbling experience. It can lead to a profound paralysis of the will: how can we simply go on living after something as monumental as this has happened? It is like a tear in the film that envelops us in everyday reality. Suddenly we are faced with the void. I can understand how people go into a deep depression as a result of such a loss.

Yet while everyone understands grief when it comes to human loss, not everyone accords the same significance to the grief that many people feel when their companion animal dies. It can be devastating, and we need to acknowledge that. Surely it is not necessary for me to say that losing a child is one of the most awful things that can happen. But in the case of dogs, and other animals as well, it is not yet self-evident, except to the people directly involved. And even they, some of them tell me, feel somewhat embarrassed at the wild grief that overcomes them when this happens.

Trying to understand the depth of despair that can overcome us leads to a recognition that our bond with animals is not just one of utility or in any way sentimental, but is something completely different that we have been, for centuries, reluctant to acknowledge. Strangely, this reluctance is paralleled by a similar reluctance to acknowledge that animals grieve for one another—and, as I will presently make clear, for us as well. It is true that we know much less about this than about our own grief, but the parallel is clear: just as we grieve for them, so they grieve for us. It is now clear that, apart from humans many other animals grieve as well, some of them almost certainly as intensely as do we (I am thinking of elephants). I am sure there has never been a time in our evolutionary history that we have not grieved for those we loved, and I believe the same is true for many wild animals. Grief is not unknown in nature any more than it is unknown in humans for our entire evolutionary history.

1

∞

Are You and Your Dog One?

Dogs and humans have a very special relationship,
where dogs have actually hijacked the human
oxytocin bonding pathway that is normally
reserved for our babies.

—BRIAN HARE

We live on the edge of a beach in Bondi, Sydney. My wife, Leila, and I walk down to the beach every morning and every evening. Whenever we go, I am always struck by the number of dogs on or off the leash walking along the grass on the edge of the beach, as they are not allowed on to the beach itself. Every once in a while, I get the feeling I am watching a film about an alien race, and the people on that planet have animals, just as we do, and those animals are on a leash just as ours are, and I think *Wow! They have this* alien *creature walking next to them, who looks up at them with friendship—sometimes even adoration—and yet is obviously under their control. But the animal, whatever kind of animal it is, does not seem to mind. How odd!* And then I realize this is exactly our situation: we have this "wild" animal, who is completely obsessed with us and who is yet alien. We do not and cannot enter into the mind of a dog. (Now lest you cat lovers begin to complain already, this early in the book, let me explain: we do not, by and large, take our cats out for walks on a leash. They would not enjoy it and we would not either. Just why this is can be explored a bit further in the book.) But it is clear that this animal at the end of a leash is enjoying herself. She is exactly where she wants to be. With us. And it is equally clear that we, too, are enjoying it. We, too, are where we want to be. Then, as Leila and I actually walk onto the clear golden sand of Bondi Beach and the half-mile walk to the end of the beach, I see a very similar scene, but this time without dogs. That scene involves small children playing in the sand, building castles, making little swimming pools with the waves as they come up, laughing and enjoying themselves immensely, just like the dogs. And their parents are taking equal pleasure—again just like with the dogs. And so I am led to think that dogs and children have a great deal in common. And some of these children are so young that we cannot, in fact, enter their minds. We do not know what they are thinking beyond knowing that they are happy and living right there in the moment. Just as dogs do. Just as we do in the presence of small children and dogs.

This is of course not astonishing, because it is an everyday experience that you, my readers, have noticed as well. And yet, it *is* actually astonishing, because the likelihood of another species enjoying our company to this extent is not something we could have predicted. For what I see when I look at the dogs is genuine happiness. There can be no doubt of it. Perhaps just ten years ago, scientists would have admonished me, "You are projecting your own feelings onto those of the dog. In fact, you cannot possibly know what emotions the dog is feeling." Of course one could make the argument, and it is popular right now, that emotions are objective, that is, they can be measured and witnessed by others, whereas feelings are internal and can only be known to the person who has them—so according to this view, we can know that an animal has emotions, but not how the animal "feels" about these emotions. I find this view somewhat artificial. I believe that nearly everyone, including those same scientists, now happily acknowledges that, yes, of course, the dog is feeling happy. Is it the same happiness that the human next to him is feeling? Well, we will never know for certain, at least in the sense that would completely satisfy a fussy philosopher, but we can be certain—I am certain—that the dog is feeling something very similar to our idea of happiness. In fact, I am willing to go further and state that the dog is feeling something *better* than, *superior* to, our happiness, because it appears to be so completely unalloyed with any other feeling. It is *pure* happiness, or that's how it appears to me. And I am willing to go still further: I think it feels that way to a *lot* of people, and that would explain why we are so eager to spend time with dogs. They give us access to a purer state of feeling than we would have without them.

Leila is a pediatrician, and I have the pleasure of watching her work from our home in Bondi. Mothers come to see her with small children—beginning with newborns and progressing until the late teens. Yes, fathers come, too, but mostly mothers do, and to keep it simple I will speak of them. By and large, and even in the face of often highly complicated illnesses that plague their children, these mothers take delight in their young. They watch them with smiles; they talk of their antics with pleasure— in short, they are in love. Part of the reason for this love is that the children are "other." It is impossible to miss this: They represent a time in our own past to which we no longer have access. Nobody remembers their earliest childhood. But we take delight in this otherness. We enjoy seeing children play with no awareness of all the problems in the world. Absorbed in themselves or in the little worlds they create or inhabit, they represent a kind of innocence that we adults may not remember, but we still long for it.

The same is true of dogs (and other animals as we shall presently see). Yes, we credit them with feelings remarkably like our own. But even when they are no longer puppies, they seem to have a more immediate access to a world of sensory happiness, one that evades us. Hence some of our species cannot bear to be without a dog. As a reminder, or as a mirror perhaps of our own evolutionary past. For surely when we were hunter-gatherers we were more like dogs than we are today. We lived in small groups spending all our time together, mostly in harmony, knowing nothing of organized warfare or the other ills that plague us today. Perhaps life was shorter than it is now—but it was probably healthier and easier. More like the lives of dogs.

To return to my morning and evening walks where I observe the happiness of dogs, it still astonishes me that this everyday occurrence is not more remarked upon as the miracle it surely is: an entirely alien creature whose mind we cannot really enter spends his time with us and loves doing so. Like something out of *Star Wars,* but actually happening right here in real time. How lovely!

I always wonder what people, should we ever make contact with a distant civilization, would want to know most. I suppose it depends on the individual: linguists would want to know how they communicate. Politicians, how they govern. Musicians, what instruments they play. IT specialists, how sophisticated their computers are—or if they are beyond our comprehension. I have to confess that I would be most curious to know—right after I found out whether they had eliminated war and interpersonal violence—what *other* creatures share their lives. Do they have the equivalent of dogs and cats, or would they consider that an imposition on the lives of other animals, as some people, even here on earth, are beginning to believe? And do they live in harmony with other creatures to the point, for example, where they would never consider eating them? This is my own bugbear as a vegan, I confess. I would certainly not be alone in my curiosity about other creatures living with aliens. Probably everybody who lives in close proximity with a dog or cat will want to know as well. We are today, as a species, pet obsessed. And that obsession is only growing.

Of course there have always been individuals who love dogs. Some more than others. But it does strike me that we are living in a very interesting time when it comes to dogs. I can remember when I wrote my book *Dogs Never Lie About Love* more than twenty years ago that, while it was immensely popular with the general public, it was decidedly less popular with academics, including zoologists, animal behavior scientists, even veterinarians, who more or less dismissed my explorations into the emotions of dogs as completely amateur and premature. But today there is hardly a university in America or Europe that does not have a *dog-cognition laboratory*. And while this is the term they use—because, I think, it sounds more scientific—in fact, they are investigating far more than the intellectual abilities of dogs. Granted, scientists have always been preoccupied (not always honorably) with just how smart "others" are, whether other creatures or even other races or other genders or classes are different from themselves. But there has never been a time until now when so many more or less hard-nosed scientists were willing to concede emotional complexity to other animals besides the human animal. Witness the popularity of such recent books as Sy Montgomery's *The Soul of an Octopus* (as well as her book *The Good Good Pig*), Helen Macdonald's *H Is for Hawk,* Jonathan Balcombe's *What a Fish Knows,* and Frans de Waal's *Mama's Last Hug.* We are so far down this path that Peter Wohlleben's book *The Hidden Life of Trees,* about the emotions and social structures of plants, has become an international bestseller of phenomenal proportions. He has also written a follow-up book about animals and, even though I wrote the preface for the U.S. edition of that book, I must admit that it does not provide the same level of astonishment that his book on trees did; a kind of intellectual epiphany that we feel when we suddenly realize there is something profound we have not ever considered before—no doubt because we are now more used to hearing about the emotional complexity of other animals.

So, to what are we to ascribe this newfound willingness to concede that humans are not the be-all and end-all of creation? Okay, that is perhaps too general a question but, at a slightly lower level, we can simply ask why dogs? And why now?

I think the answer is actually quite simple: in the last few years—maybe ten at the most—our awareness of how much coevolution there has been between the two species, humans and dogs, has made great strides. Until very recently, the general scientific consensus was that dogs were the first animal to be domesticated, but only about 10,000 to 15,000 years ago, more or less at the same time as plants became domesticated and farmed. But this date keeps getting pushed back by any number of serious scientists involved in such research, so that now the consensus is rather that dogs were domesticated some 25,000 years ago. Certain scientists are going even further and suggesting that it may have been almost 35,000 years ago. Now just a few years more and we come to 50,000 years, which is the generally accepted date for the beginning of our modern species, that is, *homo sapiens sapiens*—one sapiens would have been more than enough—which would mean that not long after we had become who we are, we associated with dogs. So it would not be surprising in the least to think that we *coevolved*—I like to believe I invented this term, just because I like it so much and it resonates so well with what I believe, but I am certain I am not even close to the first*—with dogs, while also having learned to love

---

* Darwin talked about the concept of coevolution with respect to flow-

them. After all, if our children love us—and they mostly do—surely part of the reason is that they depend on us. With dogs it goes further, because the dependency is mutual. We do not depend on children but, when we were a young species, we may well have depended on dogs: they guarded our sleeping quarters—and still do—and often even gave up their lives to protect us. What did they get in return? Not as much as they gave us, I would say, because a dog, as a wolf in a previous incarnation, was perfectly capable of getting its own food, of keeping warm by itself, of procreating and having friends and a society in which the family felt secure. We did not give them this. But we did give them something else—our affection. Why did they want it so badly? I am not sure I have the answer, because dogs are just as affectionate with one another as with us. It is not even like cats, some of whom prefer our company to that of other cats. Rare is the dog who does not want to be with other dogs and who does not enjoy romping and running and playing with them. Indeed, let's be modest here: we can never be as good a companion to a dog as another dog. I can remember times when my dog would look at me with a certain condescension as

---

ers and insects, and Paul Ehrlich first used the actual term *coevolution* in 1964 but not with respect to dogs. The journal *Nature Communications* on May 14, 2013, mentions that a team found coevolution in several brain processes—for instance, in genes that affect the processing of the brain chemical serotonin.

I chased him, obviously aware that I was no match for his canine companions. But he was kind about it.

Here is a somewhat wild conjecture: could it be that just as we like to think of ourselves as friends with an alien species, that dogs think like this, too? We couldn't do what dogs could do, but we were "other" and maybe dogs found that intriguing, just as we do.

But puzzles remain to be solved. Dogs don't just love us or want to be with us when we are kind and affectionate to them. It is a well-known paradox that a dog loves even the "master"—no doubt this is how some humans think of themselves—who hits or hurts or abuses. Later, in my chapter on going vegan, I try to understand how some societies still eat dogs (hunter-gatherers in the past almost certainly did so, if not routinely then at least when it proved necessary), when dogs seem so much a part of our society, not just here, but in Vietnam and Korea and China and any other country where some dogs are companions and others are on the menu. I am not interested for the moment in finding out how humans can bring themselves to treat dogs in this way (probably because I don't have the answer), but rather in asking the much harder question: how do dogs respond? They do not seem to fight back. They do not really make an attempt to escape into the wild to revert to being wolves or at least join a feral dog pack. They seem to meekly accept their fate. Except that we do not really know what goes on in the mind of a dog awaiting slaughter. It is not a place we want to go. Certainly I don't. But it is worth considering whether dogs have been conditioned to trust us so completely that they cannot, until the very last moment, believe that we have betrayed them.

But, even in countries where eating dogs has been traditional for centuries, major change is afoot. China, Vietnam, and South Korea all have animal rights groups that campaign against the killing and eating of dogs, and these groups are growing in strength from day to day. These same countries, again quite recently, have altered their view of dogs and it is not uncommon to see, even in small villages, dogs who are clearly treated as companions, even members of the family.

So my position is that we have reached a tipping-point when it comes to dogs, and we will not return to the days when they were considered as just a possession without interests of their own. I think this is a wonderful thing.

In trying to understand how this happened, I came across a fascinating account of wolves and an indigenous fishing people in Newfoundland, the Beothuk, who did not, it now appears, "own" dogs. They were, on the contrary, familiar with wolves, and in a way that tells us something profound about dogs, wolves, friendship, humans, and violence. Consider the following astonishing account, given by a seventeenth-century naval captain, Sir Richard Whitbourne. He had been in command of one of the warships in the naval force that fought against the "invincible" Spanish Armada, the 130 ships that set sail from Spain to invade England. The Armada was defeated in 1588 by Sir Francis Drake in what is considered one of the greatest naval battles in history. Asked by William Vaughan to govern "his" colony at Renews in Newfoundland, Whitbourne did so from 1618 until 1620. Newfoundland at the time was inhabited by these hunter-gatherers known as Beothuk. At the time of initial European contact in the seventeenth century, there may have been no more than 500 to 700 of them. They lived in independent, self-sufficient, extended family groups of 30 to 55. They were, much as the Moriori (who were conquered by the more warlike Māori) in New Zealand were, an almost completely peaceable community. Unlike many indigenous people, they refused to accept guns when these were offered in trade. And so for centuries they were hunted for fun. In 1829 they were officially declared extinct.

In 1620 Whitbourne published a book, *A Discourse and Discovery of New-found-land,* in order to promote colonization on the island. It has been assumed that the Beothuk had dogs, but in fact initially they did not. What they had were friendly wolves. Or rather, undoubtedly because of their attitude toward the wolves, they were able to establish a kind of relationship that would eventually become the protocol for turning wolves into dogs.

Here is Whitbourne's account of the relationship between the Beothuk and the wolf of Newfoundland:

> For it is well known that they are a very ongenious [sic] and subtile kind of people (as it hath often appeared in divers things), so likewise are they tractable, as hath been well approved, when they have been gently and politically dealt withall; also they are a people who will seek to revenge any wrongs done unto them, or their wolves, as hath often appeared. For they mark their wolves in the ears, with several marks, as is used here in England on sheep, and other beasts, which hath been likewise well approved; for the wolves in these parts are not so violent and devouring as those in other countries, for no man that I ever heard of, could say that any wolf . . . did set upon any man or boy.

Now if this is a true account—and why should it not be— we learn something astonishing: these people were able to treat wild wolves in much the way we treat dogs today. This is important to me because it is something I have tried to understand in several of my books, but most especially in my last book: *Beasts: What Animals Can Teach Us About the Origins of Good and Evil*. I was trying to understand just why it should be that we have an adversarial relationship with all the so-called other—other than us, that is—apex predators of the world, including wolves. One exception though is the killer whale or orca. So far there has been no instance of an orca killing a human in the wild, even though we have killed them by the thousands. Is this enmity "natural"? I suggest it is not. It is artificial, created by circumstances of our own making. What we normally have are accounts of enmity between humans and wolves going back centuries. In Norway, where apparently a wolf has neither killed nor injured anyone for the past two hundred years, and where a hunter killed the nation's last known wolf in 1966 (in 2016 there were 68 wolves in the country with the government wanting to kill 47 of them), half of the entire population responded to a recent questionnaire by saying that they are "very much afraid of wolves." In other words, it is just a deeply rooted prejudice that has persisted in spite of it being completely illogical, and unsupported by any evidence.

Douglas Smith, the leader of the Yellowstone Wolf Project in Yellowstone National Park, writes to me that there were no attacks by wolves on humans between 1995—when they were first introduced to the park—and 2009, when the study was completed.

All we can say is that we are almost uniquely fortunate that a wild species, the wolf, decided, at some point and for somewhat mysterious reasons, to throw in his lot with us, and in the bargain exposed us to a love that is perhaps unique between any two species. It is that uniqueness, surely, that makes the death of the dog so deeply painful to us.

2

∞

Their Only Fault:
Dying Before We Are Ready

Dogs have given us their absolute all. We are the
center of their universe. We are the focus of their
love and faith and trust. They serve us in return
for scraps. It is without a doubt the best deal man
has ever made.

—ROGER CARAS

Dogs get old of course. But do they get old and demented?
By the way, "demented" is a word I would love to see
retired—it has a nasty ring to it. Perhaps they get confused, or they become so old that they do not seem like
their old selves. But I believe they have more resilience
than do older humans, perhaps because they are, after all,
just wolves in dogs' clothing (even if this is not entirely
scientifically accurate). Wolves, it would appear, do not
experience dementia. Perhaps this is because they don't
live long enough, or perhaps, once they are showing signs

of cognitive decline, they are not able to participate sufficiently in pack life to maintain their position and are
"abandoned" by their pack mates—all these perhapses
show how little we really understand the life cycle of just
about *any* wild animal. But I think the reason there is so
little obvious dementia in dogs is that they usually, under
the best of circumstances, lead lives without the anxieties
that plague humans. One of these causes of anxiety of
our species is our vaunted ability to foresee the future.
I am not immune. At seventy-nine, I suddenly find myself
thinking about matters that until recently I read about
but did not consider relevant to me personally. I mean
growing old and becoming incapacitated in some form or
other, and in particular, mental deterioration. I have traveled so far down this unlikely route that I asked Simone,
my daughter, who is a nurse practitioner and whose job it
is to diagnose people with possible dementia, to give me
the test she administers to them. I am relieved to say that
I got full marks.

Why now? Well, I live with a much younger wife and
we have two sons aged eighteen and twenty-three. I cannot
bear the thought of becoming a burden to them. I would
much rather behave like a cat and wander off by myself to
die alone and unnoticed. Well, not actually die—just live,
say in a small village in Thailand near Chiang Mai, where
I could enjoy the sunshine and Thai food and the friendly
people, and hardly be noticed. My family could visit me

once a year, and that way I would not feel that my decline was having such a negative impact on their lives. Not just cats, but some though not all other "wild" animals do the same. We can only speculate why: perhaps to keep the group from suffering the ills of a single member?* But while I say this, and it is a good conversation starter at boring dinner parties, I must admit that I don't really believe it. I do not think Leila would ever leave me by myself in Thailand or anywhere else. Nor do I believe that, if she did, I would adjust and be perfectly happy. Nor do I believe that my three children would permit it either. So it is really just a fantasy of not becoming a bother in old age—one, I am sure, shared by many people my age. This is yet another reason why I am opposed to euthanasia for the aged: They might well ask for it simply because they do not want to be a burden for their family. But this is no reason to die. And if someone truly is a burden to their family or the family believes this, whether it is true or not, then surely my fantasy about Thailand is preferable to a trip to Switzerland for euthanasia.

If you go online, there is not a great deal of literature about canine dementia, and what is there is not entirely convincing or scientific. I have looked at videos online

---

* I find it interesting that of all domesticated animals, only dogs will run to us when they are frightened. Horses and cats will run away. I have seen this happen many times with my many cats: it is as if in an emergency they revert back to their wild forebears.

showing what appears to be a dog with dementia, but all you see is a small old dog wandering around the garden in circles. Since this is familiar territory to the dog, perhaps he is just repeating what he has always done and taking pleasure in the familiarity of it all.

I am not sure, then, why cats want to be by themselves when they die, at least some of them, but when it comes to dogs, one thing is clear: No dog is worried that he or she is a burden to their human family. All they want is to be constantly in touch with their family. So much so that an anonymous veterinarian recently posted a comment that has been widely shared: He said that many people find it unbearable to be present at the final moment with their dog, and they leave the room. What he sees then is that the dog frantically looks from face to face of the people present, searching for his own family, and how distressed the dog is at not finding them, and how distressed he, the vet, is by the absence of the human as well. He begs them to reconsider, even if it causes them suffering, a willingness to witness their dog's final moments. I agree with him. We owe them this comfort in their last moments, no matter how unhappy it makes us feel.

As for dementia in cats, I have found even less information than for dogs. Having had many cats in my life (see my book *The Nine Emotional Lives of Cats*) I cannot remember any cat of mine developing anything resembling dementia. I did notice though that as my cats aged, they became less interested in hunting, and I was delighted. I foolishly believed this was because I had so often admonished them and pleaded with them to stop. The cats always looked at me with a disdainful expression that translated to, "You think you're talking to someone who cares?" as they wandered out of the house in search of prey. It is also true that, as my cats matured, they became less and less interested in even leaving the house. They were "content"—the dominant word in cat language— to sit on the windowsill soaking up the sun, or to lie on a human lap, purring at high volume. At night, as they grew older, they invariably wanted to sleep in our bed, which fortunately both Leila and I considered an honor and a privilege. In winter, they even snuggled under the covers to keep warm and provide warmth to us. I could see no signs of anything that resembled dementia.

Our cats were always indoor/outdoor cats. There is a controversy over this at present: statistics show that indoor cats live on average 11 years (between 10 and 16, but they can live up to 20), whereas cats who regularly go outdoors live less than 5. This is why most cat shelters in the United States will not allow you to adopt a cat unless you agree to keep them indoors. This is a complication when it comes to the longevity of cats. Most of us who love them cannot bear the thought of their never experiencing the outdoors, and we provide them with a cat door, sometimes called the greatest human invention of all time, that allows them to explore the neighborhood. Surely, we reason, a cat needs access to the natural world and cannot possibly thrive in a permanent indoor environment? This makes intuitive sense. After all, the trade-off for a cat, in choosing domestication, should not be incarceration. But it is contradicted by the many studies that show that cats who regularly go outdoors have the shorter lifespan.* Rare is the cat who has developed a healthy respect for cars. So if we love spending years and years with our cats and growing old together, it is, alas, better to keep them from the dangers of a world they did not evolve to live in—nor did we. By the way: cars kill an inordinate number of people, too.

Now I understand the reasoning—and it is compelling—but for an animal who in the wild is constantly on the go, to be confined to a house is unnatural. The cats who do show some signs of what veterinarians call "feline cognitive dysfunction syndrome" are invariably indoor-living

---

* Outdoor cats are often, in fact, very often when they are young, hit and killed by cars; attacked by dogs and other animals; killed by sick humans who hunt them for fun; the list is endless. On the other hand, an indoor cat is often bored, gets fat and lazy, has no chance to exercise its normal behavior, and so on. The majority of veterinarians believe cats should be kept indoors. Statistics vary, but it is absolutely certain that indoor cats live far longer. See https://www.americanhumane.org/fact-sheet/indoor-cats-vs-outdoor-cats/. True, one vet in England wrote: "Indeed, outdoor cats who live beyond 1 year have a life expectancy into the high teens—just like indoor cats." But in England they have almost no natural predators whereas in the United States there are many.

cats, so I would suggest that some of this decline may not be biological, but rather a function of limited experience. The cats are probably seriously bored. This is why so many cat people living in apartments and homes where the cats do not go outside now have "catios," which are patios designed especially for cats, or they create spaces where the cat can watch the outside word from a ledge, and ledges lead to other ledges, some high, some low, with surprises along the way. I think it is a great idea to allow your imagination to run free, devising lively attractions for your feline companions. There is no reason why you cannot enrich the environment for your cat in exactly the same way you would for your child. Playing with your cat is good for you and good for the cat. My cats loved playing predator and prey, where they, naturally, were the predator and I the prey. So they would lie in wait for me as I came around the corner, and then leap out and attack my ankles. That they knew this was a game was obvious. It was also clear to me that by playing this game I could observe a cat's sense of humor. They found it funny to waylay me and pounce as if I were a mouse. It was fun and funny to them. I must say it was to me as well. Ambushing me was definitely my cats' favorite game. We were lucky to live on a beach where there were no cars, and so at night when the beach was deserted, we would go for walks and they would play the ambush game with me and with our dog as well. I am not sure he got the joke, but the cats certainly did.

We do not consider abandoning our dogs or cats simply because they have forgotten to use the litter box—not pleasant, I agree—or wander aimlessly about the house, or meow seemingly for no reason. In any case, we hardly understand cat meows—they are still awaiting interpretation. I am convinced that one day we actually will be in a position to understand what they are trying to tell us and will not believe how stupid we were *not* to have understood. There are many bad reasons for euthanasia of animal companions, and I will elaborate on this in a later chapter. For now let me simply state the obvious: the *only* reason to take a dog or cat in to the vet for euthanasia is when *they* (not us) are unbearably suffering with absolutely no prospect of cure. I think of it this way: if they could speak, would they request or rather beg us to keep them longer with their beloved family? Part of our problem is that we are not in a position to determine what happens around death in the wild, it remains a topic that has been very little studied and hence little understood.

In fact, we understand the behavior of wild animals around death very imperfectly, if at all. Witness the orca mother near Victoria, British Columbia, who, after seventeen months of gestation, gave birth to a female calf only to watch her die within a few hours, probably because the mother was malnourished—there is little wild salmon left in the area because of overfishing. The orca carried her dead infant with her for sixteen days, something never seen before—which does not mean it doesn't happen, only that we have not observed it. Whenever the baby slipped away from her and sank, the mother retrieved her from the deep. It is impossible for us to know exactly what she was feeling at the time. Nor can we be certain what she knew: It is not impossible that the mother knew that no baby whale had been born to the pod for the past three years.

Clearly this is not unlike the profound grief that humans feel at the loss of a newborn child. The researchers observing from Washington State were aware of this. Deborah Giles, a killer whale biologist with the University of Washington Center for Conservation Biology, told *The Washington Post,** "If you're a whale or a dolphin, it means that you have to go down and pick that animal up as it's sinking, bring it to the surface, hold your breath for as long as you can and then basically dump your baby off your head in order just to take a breath." Giles was watching from a research boat and said "J35 managed to do this repeatedly, all the while fighting a strong current." She added that it was likely the mother orca had not eaten in days. The mother's dedication is a testament to the strong bonds that social animals such as orcas form with their offspring. "It's real, and it's raw," Giles said. "It's obvious what's happening. You cannot interpret it any other way.

---

* Chiu, Allyson. "An Orca Calf Died Shortly after Being Born. Her Grieving Mother Has Carried Her Body for Days." *Washington Post,* WP Company, July 27, 2018.

This is an animal that is grieving for its dead baby, and she doesn't want to let it go. She's not ready." This reaction is similar to how many people feel when they lose a child, Giles continued. "That's part of what people are picking up on like, my God, I would feel the same way if I had a baby that only took a couple of breaths. I wouldn't want to let it go either." But orcas are far more mysterious beings to us than dogs. We are on much firmer ground when it comes to dogs, both because of the length of the time we have lived together, and also because of the intensity of the bond (nobody has ever lived with a wild orca; in fact, nobody has ever witnessed a wild orca giving birth).

Dogs generally don't do what the big cats do, that is, wander off to die alone. I suspect the reason is that dogs are too much like us. Having lived with us for tens of thousands of years, they have become like us even when faced with death. That is sheer hypothesis, I agree, but it makes sense. There is further evidence: There are some dogs who grow old along with their human companions. A friend who was in the early stages of dementia told me that as she began to notice her own still fairly benign cognitive decline, she became aware that her dog, not yet ten, was beginning to show signs of mental aging as well. She wondered whether this was in fact biological, or perhaps something else, which she called "contagious empathy." She believed that her dog felt her needs so acutely that as she began her slow decline, he wanted to decline with her—to keep her company as it were. I don't believe it was real dementia.

And note here something we can learn about how to treat humans from the way we treat dogs: I have not come across a single person (which of course does not mean that such people do not exist) who has told me that they want to give their dog to a home for old dogs, just because the dogs are indeed getting old. Everyone I know in such a situation wants to take care of their dog at home. I believe this is the dog's preference, too, and it is almost certainly the preference of nearly every human with dementia who is not at home, but in a public or private facility. I understand that for various reasons people often have no choice, but it still seems to me far from ideal.

I am watching from a distance as my dog Benjy, at thirteen, begins his decline. I would not call what he has dementia, but clearly his mental state is not as acute as it once was. The main symptom of aging is that he has become incontinent in the apartment (he has no immediate access to a garden). Ilan is taking care of him in Berlin while we are in Sydney, although we visited a few months ago for a month. Benjy does not appear very concerned about his incontinence. He just goes as if he were outside. Ilan does not make a fuss and cleans it up. Interestingly, instead of a fully fledged bowel movement, more often Benjy leaves little date-like cubes, almost as a polite gesture—"I had to go, but I tried to make them as benign as possible." He doesn't appear confused. Most important of all, his ability to love has not declined in the least. He sleeps in Ilan's bed at night, and I have told Ilan that if he finds a girlfriend and she objects to this arrangement, he needs a different girlfriend. Benjy puts his head on Ilan's chest and stares up at my son's face with pure love. He is experiencing as he always has, delight in being with his closest friend.

Friends tell me that when their dogs decline, it is usually a physical thing: they can no longer go for walks; they defecate in the house; they lose their appetite; they appear to be in pain when walking. But it is rare that anyone tells me their dog is declining mentally, and never yet have I heard that a dog has lost the capacity to feel love. One friend though, who had a dog named Sima, tells me of a possible exception. Toward the end of her life, Sima no longer wanted to cuddle. It broke the heart of her human companion, since Sima would only ask for a cuddle as a pretext for wanting to go outside in the middle of the night (later in this book I quote the whole story of Sima, since she had been my dog, too). I also heard from another friend whose dog was mortified by defecating in the house, so they put down paper and the dog used it. On the last day of her life, a vet came to put her down, and as she lay dying, she had a last bout of diarrhea, and managed to crawl to the paper for the last time.

The great question, for which a definitive answer is

probably not likely, is whether dogs think about their death. Do they have any conception of it? I am not going to play expert here, because I don't really believe anyone knows the answer. Many people have had experiences that would suggest answers, but these vary widely. I am sure that dogs do not, unlike me, spend a lot of time while they are still perfectly healthy, wondering what will happen when they are not. They do not, I am certain, wonder what life will be like after death (a strange phrase, I admit). Or, put another way, they do not wonder whether there is an afterlife, or whether they will experience anything at all after they are dead. I remember my father, Jacques, who was born in France, telling me shortly before he died at eighty-four that he was very curious to learn what would happen after he died. It is not as if he believed that anything in particular would happen, but he was almost happy at the thought of dying so that at last he would know. This is yet another strange use of language—because of course he would not know if there were nobody to do the knowing. When we write about death, or even think about it using language, we are very soon in novel territory. It is like trying to imagine the nothingness that comes right after death: How do you even find words for this? How does our mind come to grips with it?

Kate Benjamin, who has teamed up with Jackson Galaxy, the cat behaviorist from the television show *My Cat from Hell,* and has been written up several times in *The New York Times,* has had breast cancer. She was featured in *The New York Times* on September 6, 2018, "As animal assisted therapy thrives, enter the cats," when she reported that just as she finished chemo, her favorite cat—she has nine—died. She told the reporter, Jennifer Kingson, "I just miss him so much. I feel like, in some sort of 'woo-woo' way, he was there for me through this, and then he was like 'O.K., you're good, I've got to go.'" I had to read that twice, the second time without tears. Quite apart from the sweet sentimentality involved, this passage does raise a critical issue, namely how much do other animals understand about their death and about our death? Not a great deal has been written about this, so I hope you will forgive the tentative nature of what follows.

Do cats and dogs somehow intuit "I am reaching the end?" If so, and I suspect that they do to some extent, they do not face that end with fear. Many humans, as they sense the approach of death, completely fall apart and become extremely fearful, anxious, even panicked. I have not heard of a dog or cat who does this. Perhaps they are able to feel something related to knowing that they will lose contact with their cherished friend. Do they in fact know this? It is very difficult to say, or to find evidence either way. Perhaps they believe the separation will only be temporary, the way many religious people feel? I wish I could share this belief. Alas, I am afraid that I cannot: I do believe that death is permanent, that there is no afterlife and that nothing of us survives, except memories in those we leave behind.

This is probably a good thing for dogs and cats, but we, their human companions, are not so blessed. And as the end approaches for our beloved animals, invariably or at least most of the time much earlier than it does for us, we are often completely devastated.

As I have indicated above, animals are like children to us and we feel so helpless when they are dying and we are not able to protect them from death. This helplessness perplexes children, dogs, cats, and even adult humans. Alas, there is nothing alive that will not die, and this is a painful truth that nobody can completely comprehend. Fortunately, we need think about it only a few times in our lives. But living with dogs and cats presents too many opportunities to do so. Would that it were otherwise.

3

∞

All Things Bright and Beautiful Must Have an End: Dying Dogs

If you have a dog, you will most likely outlive it; to get a dog is to open yourself to profound joy and, prospectively, to equally profound sadness.

—MARJORIE GARBER

Dogs normally die when they are between seven and twenty years old, depending on their size. Nobody is sure why, but it is probably linked to selective breeding. A Great Dane for example has to grow to a hundred times its birth weight in the first year. Nothing like this happens in the wild. Unlike humans, there is not a huge variation depending on the lives the dogs lead. So small poodles will probably reach at least fourteen, whereas the larger breeds rarely live past twelve, with the average age at death for a Great Dane, for example, being seven. In spite of this, I can't help but wonder if Bernese Mountain Dogs lead particularly short lives, because of what they do or how large they are.

This does not seem to be true of other animals: whales and elephants lead very long lives, whereas tiny mice live short ones. The bowhead whale, which is pretty big (65 tons and sixty feet long), can live as long as two hundred years! Nor is it true of cats, perhaps simply because there is not a great size differential. The largest cats, Maine Coons, are big (the males are 12–18 pounds; females 10 or less—probably they are so large because they evolved in cold-weather northern countries where their heavy fur was useful for walking in snow) but the variation is not enormous in comparison to dogs: a small dog can weigh less than 5 pounds, and big dogs can reach 150 pounds.

I had a tendency when I was younger to believe that very tall humans have shorter lives than smaller ones, but this was just based on anecdotes—and the fact that I am not very tall. There is little science behind it. On the other hand, obviously there is an enormous discrepancy in size between humans. Less obviously, men, on average, die younger than women. Men are also much more likely than women to die prematurely, and this is particularly true, according to the World Health Organization (WHO), in countries with strong gender disparity. The more equitable the country in terms of men and women, the longer the men live. But this social origin of aging is not true of dogs: Female dogs also live slightly longer, on average, than male dogs. Is this related to aggression? Possibly, because dogs live longer when they are neutered. That applies to male and female dogs. It seems to me that large male dogs are somewhat more aggressive than large female dogs, but I am not certain this has been sufficiently researched. (Among animals in general, with few exceptions, such as hyenas, males tend to be more aggressive than females.)

Almost everyone who lives with a dog or cat will experience their death, because of their shorter life span. As we have seen in the preceding chapters, we are simply not prepared for this. We rant and rail and curse fate. We want our beloved companions to live longer. This is especially true of people with dogs. Maybe they don't want their dogs to live as long as the big parrots, many of whom will survive long past our own death, but certainly as long as cats. According to *The Guinness Book of World Records,* the oldest cat for whom records exist lived to the age of 38, but even the average age is still much longer than for dogs, between 12 and 15. The longest-lived dog was 29.

Because dogs and cats stand to us in particular in a child-adult relationship, losing them is very much like losing a child. I know I repeat this often, but that is because it is so essential to our understanding of how we relate to dogs and cats, and other animal companions. People who do not recognize this relation are puzzled and sometimes even hostile to people who cherish their dogs and cats. Karl Ove Knausgaard, for one, recently published an article in *The New Yorker* against writers and dogs—perhaps he was joking, but he asked, "Has a single good author ever owned a dog?" And his answer was "No." (Forgetting Virginia Woolf, Ernest Hemingway, Kurt Vonnegut, and even Freud who was also a fine author.) His point seems to have been that there was only room for one solipsist in the house, forgetting that dogs are anything but self-preoccupied; they are more like us-preoccupied.

In some sense, the sudden death of a dog or cat seems to go against the natural order. Or rather, that is how it feels to us emotionally. Why? Because these animals are so dependent on us and so vulnerable, and because they have done nothing to deserve a death that we consider early. But also, consider how much time we spend with these animals: the entire time we are at home, we are in their presence. We go for solitary walks with our dogs, sometimes for hours. We may not even realize it, but we confide in them. They never criticize us; they never look at us in disbelief ("I cannot believe you just said that! How can you be such a jerk?"). No human companion is as understanding, as forgiving, as eager to be in your presence. You can cuddle your wife or husband for an hour, but a cat will lie on your lap all afternoon. A dog will lie at your feet all day if necessary, until you give in and take her out.

So there is a unique intimacy in both cases. If your dog is well socialized and bonded to you, as usually happens, this intimacy will be without conflict. The emotional tone does not change. In fact, while this bonding ritual takes place, we are living in their space, because this is just how these animals relate to their companions in the wild. Well, maybe I am exaggerating here—we don't actually know all that much about the intimate daily interactions of the big cats, or even wolves. Nobody has lived long-term on intimate terms with a wild animal in the wild and in their own environment, and probably never will for the simple reason that we are not them, but, when they live with us, they are more or less us. The exceptions that exist, often interesting, involve people who have raised a wild animal from infancy—wolves, for example—or the extraordinarily intimate relationship a man forged with wild bears. I write about this later in this book.

When I was in Berlin I met a remarkable woman who was working on solutions to pollution around the world. She occupies a high position and is one of the leaders in the field. I told her about the book I was writing, and her eyes filled with tears. Tell me, I begged her, why are you crying. She told me the following story about her dog Jack, and then I understood completely. I think it is very brave of her to tell this story, but I also believe doing so will help other people in such a situation. I am honored to be able to include it here:

I had a farm in Africa . . . better, I had a friend who had a farm in Africa. A beautiful farm bordering a national park, surrounded by hills and lying near a river; elephants and hippos were our neighbors. And I had a dog, Jack, a truly African dog: always happy and hungry and ready to run. When we arrived at the farm, I would let him out of the car and he would race my Toyota until we reached the gates of the house. He loved those runs and I loved watching him pushing forward on the dusty road, under an African sun, and then rush to drink and cool down under an acacia.

But darkness was never far away and these days full of sun we filled with drinks and drugs, to muffle the voice of a deep malaise inside.

And so it happened that one of those days of sun and shadows, drinks and drugs, my friend was driving and Jack was running. The noise of Jack's spine as it broke against the wheels of the jeep is still inside my head. I jumped out of the moving car and held my arms out. Jack was moving forward and watching me with an expression of pain, fear and confusion. He just made it in my arms and died.

I buried him at the farm in a little grave I dug that night under a baobab. With him I buried that part of myself that had allowed this to happen:

the weak, indecisive, self-destructive and irresponsible me.

The pain and shame for having caused the death of Jack in such an incredibly stupid manner was the turning point for me: it took me a year to "clean myself" up and end that life style, but I did, and I never went back. Every time it got difficult, I remembered that sunny, horrible day and the question in my dog's eyes: why? Today I know that Jack saved my life.

Children especially will say, "she was my best friend." They mean it. They mean, I think (if I remember my own feelings about this correctly, when I lived as a child with dogs and cats) *that they were able to tell the animal everything—that is everything they never told anyone else.* And of course they did not get any criticism for telling. They did not have an argument. They did not get a lecture. There was not even a raised eyebrow. They were not told to "wait until your father comes home." There was no "I am shocked" or "I am so disappointed in you." The child knows that the animal cannot express any of these things but also believes that such ideas could never cross their mind. They feel that their animal clearly has nothing to criticize, sees nothing in them that is not loveable. There is no negative judgment. Who would not like such a relationship?

The subtle film *The Other Side of Hope* by the Finnish filmmaker Aki Kaurismäki, does not push its message—so much so that if you don't pay attention closely you will miss the point. There is a scene where a manager of a restaurant comes in, sees a dog the employees are trying to hide, and tells them the dog must go by the next day. We expect something else to happen regarding the dog. It does not. Until the very final scene of the film where, for a split second, we see the "hero," the refugee, feel a first glimmer of hope for the future and, at that very instant, the same dog appears and licks his face. So we know in a flash that the dog will be with him for life. The hope of the film is the dog who brings joy to the man when hardly anything else does. The filmmaker knows that and knows that you know it, too. How astonishing that we who live with dogs *all* know that.

As I have discussed this topic with friends, I have become aware of two very separate facts: one is that many people are scandalized that some people bond more closely with a companion animal than with a member of their own family. A famous case is Mozart: three years after buying a starling, evidently for musical reasons because he liked her song, Mozart organized an elaborate funeral for her. The scandal was that his own father had died just a few weeks before the death of the starling, and Mozart organized no such funeral. The popular blogger Lee Kynaston, wrote a much-read piece in the *Daily Telegraph* in England in which he said that the death of his cat affected him as deeply as the death of his father. He writes, convincing me:

That night I could not stop crying. I was certainly not prepared for the cavernous depth of my grief. In truth, the pain of losing this small, black and white animal, who'd been part of my life since the turn of the millennium, was every bit as intense as that of losing my father to cancer back in 1997. Now that's a controversial thing to say, I know. And to begin with I was wracked with guilt for even thinking such a thing. And yet, it's true. When you tell people this, many of them tend to think you're heartless, disrespectful or just plain nuts. After all, how can you possibly compare the death of a pet—a mere animal—to the death of a loved one? Well, quite easily as it happens, because the animal in question was a loved one, too.

I am aware, as I read about dogs, that the word that occurs most, without a single exception that I know of, is the word "love," at least in memoirs about life with a particular dog. Odd that such an abstract term, which can mean so many different things to so many different people, is invariably evoked when it comes to dogs. They seem to love us without any kind of boundary. It is odd, because in some ways it is so unexpected that it can come as a shock to the system. We are not prepared for this because, unless we have already been exposed to it, it seems unlikely, even unreal. I have a close friend and I can still remember the day I first met him and his wife. This was in Auckland, New Zealand, and the wife asked me what I did. I said I was writing a book about cats, about how complex their emotional lives were, and she responded "Who gives a shit?" I was, I admit, taken aback, as much by the sentiment as by the frank and casual manner in which it was delivered. We had just been introduced, and this was the first thing she said to me. I forgave her nearly immediately, because she was an astonishingly intelligent woman and her field was children. How could I find fault with somebody who devoted her life to fighting for the rights of children? She just had no place in her life—or her heart—for animals. Yet, in spite of the unpromising beginning, we became friends. That was twenty years ago. Yesterday I received an email with a photo and, yes, you guessed—her latest love is a new puppy whom she finds irresistible.

So, yes, it is easy to make converts to loving a dog. We love them, very much as we love other members of our family (and sometimes more because they almost never annoy us), but unlike what happens with other family members, we often have to leave our dogs. This is not easy. There are times when it is necessary to hand your dog over to someone who will love them with the same ferocity you do. You may be going to a country where it is difficult to bring a dog, or you may be in some other situation where it is simply impossible to keep your dog. In such cases, I recommend that you *never* leave them at a shelter. That is because you cannot be certain they will be rehomed, and even if you are sure, you cannot know what that home will be like. The only acceptable alternative is to find a good friend whom you trust and who loves dogs and your dog in particular and see if they are willing to take your beloved friend. This is what happened to me once with my dog Sima. Here is her story *after* she left our house and went to live with my friend Jenny Miller.*

Jenny writes:

My soulmate dog companion was Sima. She appeared to be Border Collie-Golden mix. Long orange fluffy hair like a Golden Retriever and a pointed Collie nose, not unlike a fox in appearance. She was exceptionally intelligent, which I understand is a trait of Border Collies, but her heart was pure Golden.

I don't remember at what point it became clear that Sima and I were destined to be soulmates. Was it the time when I found out I had been turned

---

* Her story from before is found in my book *Dogs Never Lie About Love*.

down for a job I really wanted, and a few tears silently trickled down my cheeks? Sima came and dropped a big meaty raw bone at my feet, the most prized and fought-over possession among Jeff's three dogs. Jeff was moving overseas, and traveling for long periods, so he asked me if I wanted Sima to live with me.

Thus began our long odyssey together. As someone who is not especially athletic, I would get great vicarious pleasure in watching Sima swim and splash after sticks in the water, and race to collect sticks in her mouth when she was on dry land. She didn't believe in the wimpy tradition of "fetch." If she chased a stick, it was now hers to keep, and if I threw ten sticks, she would collect all ten in her mouth. This habit may have actually saved her life once.

For a while we lived in a small conservative Northern California town, where many people cruelly abused their dogs by leaving them chained up outside. Sima and I always passed one such dog on our walks to the nearby wild space. The dog would bark and growl ferociously as if he wanted nothing better than to tear us limb from limb, but the chain prevented him from taking action.

One day, after her usual workout chasing sticks in the open space, Sima simply refused to drop them.

I always insisted she leave the sticks there since eventually, she would run out of sticks to chase if she brought them all home as she would have preferred. On this one occasion, she refused to drop them and nothing I could say or do would induce her to. She had very powerful jaws, and an equally powerful stubborn streak, so I gave up and let her keep her prized collection as we started home. As usual, we passed the ferocious dog, but this time, his chain broke and he came tearing up, growling and ready to attack. Sima was never a slouch when it came to defending herself, but there was no way she was going to drop those sticks. She stood there impassively, holding them in her mouth. The dog was confused. What good is a dogfight if one person refuses to fight? He wandered away.

As Sima grew into her elder years and began developing joint problems, my attention to her health grew more focused. I would cook her organic meals and give her the best supplements that money could buy. When her hips finally did seem to fail, I would take her to a genius chiropractor many miles away, who mainly worked on humans, but treated animals on the sly. She would recover.

Inevitably, as time passed, Sima's health began to dramatically deteriorate. She started peeing in the house, so I found a rare human remedy for this problem and it worked for Sima. I got even more expensive and effective joint supplements, like the holistic one that was used for racehorses.

One day we went for our normal walk and her hind legs were all twisted up as if she were in agony. At that moment, I knew. I knew, even though every atom of my being was screaming No! It was [as] if the earth had suddenly slipped on its axis. I knew that she would not be around much longer. Very soon after this, she stopped being willing to go for walks. Although she received the best western and alternative veterinary care possible, she was not going to get better. She became incontinent again and usually was not willing to even stand up.

Every once in a while, Sima's condition would suddenly improve and she would be able to walk. It was on one such day when Sima's final appointment with the vet occurred. Jeff had suggested calling his daughter Simone for help, who at the time was working as a veterinary assistant. I like to think it reassured Sima to see her old friend from childhood at this alien place. My friend Elsbeth insisted on meeting us there, which I will always treasure as a great act of friendship.

I could tell the vet was a bit taken aback, since Sima was still mobile, that I felt this final action was necessary. I was too heartbroken to talk, but Elsbeth explained—Sima had been in extreme pain, took no pleasure in life, and I was having to move out of my house soon, so she would not have a safe and comfortable environment for her final days, even if they could be extended a few weeks.

There was no way around it.

They gave Sima a tranquilizer and she lay quietly. When the time came for the final shot, I told the vet, "Let her sniff your hand, so she knows you're a friend." The shot was given and seconds later the tears, which had thus far evaded me, came gushing from my eyes.

For the next few days, I felt light and happy, glad that Sima was out of her pain and suffering. The grieving took hold later and didn't leave me, even years later. I wouldn't think about her for weeks at a time, and then something would remind me of her. I still can't go for walks in the places where she used to play her ecstatic "fetching is for wimps" game.

I am so glad that I found such a loving home for Sima as this passage makes abundantly clear.

I would hazard the guess that if you had asked people some twenty years ago to name the capacity that distinguishes humans from other animals, the answer would have been love. Most people did not believe that other

animals were capable of love, either for us or for one another. I am not sure why this has changed so dramatically,
but it has. In fact, I am willing to go even further and suggest that there are now a considerable number of people
who believe that some animals are capable of greater love
than we are. Of course I am thinking of dogs. Or let me
try to put it in a different way: dogs are capable of a different kind of love, one unalloyed with ambivalence. I know
that this has been said many times, but I think every time
anyone becomes aware of this it is like a bolt from the
blue: how can it be possible that some *other* animal is capable of something I am not? Sometimes we are suddenly
faced with the incontrovertible fact that someone else is
more talented than we are. They sing better. They are
smarter. They think more deeply. They are a better artist. They are more athletic. They are kinder. But if somebody told you that there are people who love far more
than you do, I think you would hesitate to believe it. So
I am sure that when people who have not lived with dogs
hear from their dog-obsessed friend that the love they feel
coming from their dog is greater than any other love they
have ever experienced, they think they are exaggerating
or wrong, or even crazy. And until you experience it, it
is hard to believe that it exists. But once you do experience it, you wonder how you managed to live without it.
By the same token, until we feel it, we have no idea that
we are capable of loving an animal companion with such

pure ferocious love as we find we do when we fall in love with a cat or dog or other animal.

The existence of this love raises difficult philosophical questions. Let's suppose for a moment that I am right and that it is a real quality that most dogs possess, both for us, and also for members of their own kind. The question then is, whence comes this love? Why should it exist? What purpose does it serve? Is there anything analogous in nature? Ah, there is the heart of the question. I find it one of the most interesting questions anyone can ask: is there something analogous to the love dogs feel in nature? I am afraid that the answer is one that will always elude us. Why? Because we do not know enough about relations, and especially love relations, in nature to answer. We see constantly and are even bombarded with instances of affection in the wild. Nobody would deny it. But how do we get from affection to love? What enables us to take that important one step further? Affection is something anyone can observe. It hardly needs a definition. Love, on the other hand, is a subjective feeling, and we can never actually answer to its existence except for ourselves. There could be strong evidence that your wife loves you, but only she really knows. So I believe that animals in the wild and our companion animals, feel love. That is how it looks to me. But it is still something of a leap into the dark. Of course birds who mate for life, and who sometimes grieve piteously over the death of their companion, must feel something similar to what we feel, and we call it love. Whales often stay together for their entire long lives—do they not feel more than plain affection? There have been careful studies of all these animals, and of course chimpanzees and bonobos, starting with the pioneer work of Jane Goodall, and most observers would, I suspect, go beyond using the word "affection" and would be comfortable with "love," but it is still a very subjective matter and one that we can never entirely settle to everyone's satisfaction. I am happy to go on the record and call it love, but I know that some scientists are not.

Take, for example, the meme of the moment on the internet: it was just reported that a young, lost (orphaned?) narwhal, the unicorn of the sea, a toothed whale from the Arctic Sea with a large protruding tusk derived from a canine tooth, has been adopted by a pod of adolescent Beluga whales. "He is one of the boys," said the scientists who observed this unusual behavior. Imagine how reluctant we would be to say that this narwhal loves the Belugas or that the Beluga whales love him in turn. We would have a very difficult time entertaining such a notion. But why? Essentially, we are unable to penetrate the emotional states of other beings, except by using our imagination, by insisting on obliterating the us/them distinction even if only momentarily so as to attempt to enter their minds or their hearts. It is not science, granted, but neither is it scientific to refuse any attempt to understand something that is so significant. True, animal scientists have been cautious, always aware that ascribing emotions and thoughts to animals can be fraught. How can we really know, they say? On the other hand, many animal researchers today agree with me that we have been overly cautious in the past, and that we need to allow our imagination more freedom. Besides, and here we return to the heart of my argument, dogs have done precisely this with respect to our species. It can be argued—or, let me put it this way, I wish to argue—that dogs in fact have developed something unique in their ability to intuit our emotional states and to show empathy. The almost universal reference to the way a dog lays his head on our thigh to look up at us gives everyone who experiences this a kind of shudder of intellectual excitement. We are witnessing something unprecedented in human history.

I am aware of the emphasis in the foregoing passages on dogs, not cats. Why is that? I think because while I have absolutely no doubt about the love that humans feel for cats, I am not quite as certain of the love that cats feel for humans. Affection, yes. Friendship, yes. But having lived for many years with both dogs and cats, I have not had the same feeling of being adored by any of my many cats. Liked, sure. I might even go so far as to say it was something like love. But still, it felt different from what I was getting from my dogs. I am trying to be honest here, but also tentative. It may be my mistake and not my cats'. Also, we need to remember that cats have only joined humans relatively recently in comparison with dogs, since we now believe that dogs' relationship to humans goes back at least 35,000 years. Cats go back a respectable 9,000 years, but still not long enough to have become a co-species as it were with humans. I have not heard anyone say we have coevolved with cats, but to say that about dogs is practically a cliché these days.

And yet, we definitely bond with cats in very deep ways, as I have noted throughout this book. And the grief we feel when they die is no less than the grief we feel for a dog. I would never say that a cat cannot become as close to a human as a dog, although many people think that, especially people who have not lived for years with a cat. And keep in mind that we generally live longer with a cat than we do with a dog, simply because cats on average live longer than dogs. So it is not unusual to find someone who has lived with her cat for twenty years or even more. The bond is intimate, and the corresponding grief is intense when death breaks it. But there may nonetheless be a difference and one that might be attributed to the more solitary nature of cats or to the perception some have that cats never *entirely* trust us the way dogs do. I am thinking of how cats die.

I may be wrong, but it seems to me that we euthanize cats in our own homes less frequently than dogs. Cats seem to die on their own, not just going somewhere by themselves for the final act as I have already referred to, but sometimes doing it in their own way, quietly, by themselves. It is as if they are not appealing to us to do something to help them go quietly into that night as seems to be the case with dogs. It is as if they already know what to do. Why would this be? I don't know, and perhaps my experience is limited and I will hear from readers with more knowledge than me. In the next chapter I look more closely at cats and death.

4

∞

Cats Know More About Death Than We Suspect

The smallest feline is a masterpiece.

—LEONARDO DA VINCI

Dogs can be trained to sniff cancer, as everyone has heard by now, with far greater accuracy than any cancer specialist's diagnosis. What we cannot know for certain is whether they feel sorry for the person whose cancer they detect. Does it make them sad, or is it simply a game to them, for which they receive a treat when they detect the disease? Hard to tell. While it is true that bomb-sniffing dogs don't attach any emotion to what they are finding, it is nonetheless the case that the dogs after 9/11 became depressed when they could no longer find signs of life. I don't think we can claim this is because the "game" became less interesting. I think they were aware that they were doing something very important for humans. Similarly, researchers wonder whether dogs could also smell an impending death. This has not been tested. Cats, on the other hand, it would appear, can smell death. Or at least one cat can. It was not determined through a test but appeared spontaneously and made international headlines.

In 2007, the New England Journal of Medicine, published a one-page article by David Dosa, a geriatrician, and assistant professor of medicine in the medical school at Brown University, entitled *A Day in the Life of Oscar the Cat*. It was an account of a two-year-old cat who had been adopted as a kitten by the Steere House Nursing and Rehabilitation Center in Providence, Rhode Island, a facility for dementia and Alzheimer patients. What grabbed international attention was the "fact" that Oscar had a strange talent, if that is what you want to call it, for wandering into the room of a patient, settling down next to his or her head, purring and waiting. For what? For the death that invariably came within hours. Oscar would visit various rooms every day but would only stay in the room of someone who was about to die. How did Oscar know? Ah, that is the question everyone wants answered. By the time the article was published in 2007, Oscar had "officiated"—it is hard to find the right words for what Oscar did and what Oscar was capable of—at the death of more than 25 patients at the facility. By 2010 that was 50, and by 2015 it was 100! He was invariably correct.

Oscar is one of six cats at the facility, and none of

the other cats have whatever we choose to call this angel of death's ability. It is a pet-friendly place, and the floor where he resides (presides over?) is a forty-one-bed unit treating people with end-stage Alzheimer's, Parkinson's, and other illnesses. The nurses there say he is not a friendly cat: he hisses at people who he thinks might want to pet him (he is on important business?) and is generally aloof. The doctors first noticed Oscar when he was merely six months old and started his calling. By the time he had sat for his twenty-fifth death, the staff knew they could call the family the minute Oscar took up his position. To all appearances Oscar was merely napping. But the staff called the family because that damn cat was always right.

Three questions immediately suggest themselves:

1. What was Oscar doing, or, even more provocatively, what did Oscar think he was doing?
2. How did Oscar do it?
3. Is it true?

To answer the third question first: As respected a medical authority as Siddhartha Mukherjee, acclaimed author of *The Emperor of All Maladies: A Biography of Cancer,* and, more recently, *The Gene: An Intimate History,* is convinced it is true.* Of course there are skeptics as well,

---

* "This Cat Sensed Death. What If Computers Could, Too?," *New York*

claiming it is just one more example of confirmation bias, that is, we want to believe it and so ignore anything that does not confirm our desire to believe—for example: how many times did Oscar nap next to somebody who was just fine the next day?

So on to question number one: What kind of cat cuddles with someone who is just about to die? A compassionate cat? An uncanny cat? An evil cat (some, few I hope, but some, surely, thought he was responsible for the death). Or just a cat who wanted a peaceful place to catnap? I have to interrupt my narrative here: Years ago I had a high fever, and the woman I was living with did not like my moaning and groaning, and sent me into a quiet hallway where I could lie and complain with nobody to hear me. Nobody but my cat Yogi (I have a tendency to use the same name over and over if I like it). Not only did Yogi hear me, but Yogi curled up on my stomach and could not be persuaded to leave me. I was thrilled (fortunately at that point I had not heard of Oscar the Cat and his notorious ability, or I would have been alarmed), taking it as proof that Yogi was a better friend than my girlfriend. (In retrospect, I believe I had a good point.) But in hindsight, and I hate to admit it, I am now willing to countenance the belief that Yogi

Times, January 8, 2018, https://www.3quarksdaily.com/3quarksdaily/2018
/01/this-cat-sensed-death-what-if-computers-could-too.html.

simply wanted a warm comfortable spot to lie in, and with my high fever, I was the warmest spot around.

So now we come to the most controversial aspect of the story: question number two. Most of the doctors who weighed in noted that Oscar would sniff the air when he entered the room, and therefore they believe he was able to detect an odor, perhaps the one emitted by dying cells, that was undetectable to humans. This is a popular explanation, because we all enjoy the thought that animals have access to knowledge that lies beyond humans. Earthquake sensors? Tsunami predictors? I am not ruling this out. But then we have to account for the fact that no other cat has ever been known to do this. I know, dog people will have a perfectly reasonable explanation: all cats can do this, but why bother?

But let's go back to Dr. Mukherjee for a moment. He ends his essay with these words:

But I cannot shake some inherent discomfort with the thought that an algorithm might understand patterns of mortality better than most humans. And why, I kept asking myself, would such a program seem so much more acceptable if it had come wrapped in a black-and-white fur box that, rather than emitting probabilistic outputs, curled up next to us with retracted claws?

In other words, yes, we can probably invent a machine that knows more about impending death than any doctor, but we don't like the idea. We want a cat to do it! And bear in mind that the algorithm could predict death within a few months. Oscar the cat's prediction was within a few hours.

So as a cat lover, yet skeptical of anyone's ability to predict death (even medical doctors) I am placed in an interesting dilemma by this story. Anyone hearing the story for the first time believes it, because it is nice to think cats possess mystic powers. And let's face it, this is pretty heady stuff, passing strange to say the least. If leading physicians and the most finely calibrated computers (fed the most sophisticated algorithms) cannot say that somebody will die on a given night, how on earth can a cat?

And if one cat, why not all cats? Or if all cats can, why don't they? And should we treat cats better and give them more respect? Yes, indeed. I like to think that cat adoptions spiked when this article first appeared. How could we allow cats to be put to death when they knew when we were going to die, and might even be persuaded to tell us, and even give us a few moments of final comfort? Besides, what's next for cats? Showing us how to avoid the death?

And if we learn that cats can take one look at us, and know when we will die, well, what then? How can we persuade them to let us know, or, even more urgent, how can we persuade them *not* to let us know? Will I now rush out and find myself a cat or will I show the door to my quietly sleeping pussy? The next time you are at a dinner party, try this tale and see what your fellow guests say. I think you will be surprised at the number of people who believe cats are our superior. I have always maintained that many animals have emotions far more powerful than our own. So it is not impossible for me to believe that cats can "sense" death and usually, being very polite beings, choose to keep it to themselves.

I have been teasing a bit, but the story really does raise some very serious and interesting questions. As previously mentioned, dogs can sniff out cancer far better than any doctor or any machine. But cancer is an illness. What is death, that Oscar can sniff it out? Does he sniff something physical, or does he just "know" that the end is nigh? And apart from taking a nap once he makes his discovery, what effect does it have on him? It is hard to know. Many would say that he doesn't care. But it is also possible that the many are wrong about cats' indifference to death, and Oscar and his fellow pussies know something that "passeth human understanding."

Yes, it is possible that Oscar knows something about death. But would it be a stretch to say he is attempting to comfort the dying? Not necessarily. But how far can we take cats and human health? Well, we can agree with medical opinion that purring has a calming effect on humans and increases their well-being. I don't think we can expect much controversy here. Leslie Lyons, the principal investigator in the Feline Genetics and Comparative Medicine Laboratory in the University of Missouri College of Veterinary Medicine notes that "the purring of a cat lowers stress—petting a purring cat has a calming effect. It decreases the symptoms of dyspnoea (difficulty in breathing) in cats and humans. It also lowers blood pressure and reduces the risk of heart disease. Cat owners have 40% less risk of having a heart attack."[*]

But what if we were to say that cats would like to save the lives of humans? Oh? Do they? Have you any evidence? Actually, there are a quite few anecdotes where cats will attempt to wake a human when a house is catching fire. Even when they have a cat door and could simply leave on their own. But how far will a cat go to help a human? Not, I am afraid, as far as a dog. There are seeing-eye dogs, but not seeing-eye cats. And I have to believe that had anyone in one of the twin towers had a cat, that cat would be gone in a flash and would not have led their human friend down the darkened stairs. As did at least two guide dogs: Roselle who guided Michael Hingson from the seventy-eighth floor, and Salty, who guided Omar Rivera from the seventy-first floor. But note that neither dog returned to those buildings to rescue others. So the viral

---

[*] Biloine W. Young, "Is There Healing Power in a Cat's Purr?," *Orthopedics This Week*, June 22, 2018.

internet story of the golden retriever named Daisy, who is supposed to have gone back three times to rescue more than 900 people from the WTC, is, alas, pure fiction. Nice story though. And to say a word for cats, there are numerous accounts of cats who braved a burning building multiple times to save their kittens. Note, kittens, not human babies.

It's not clear that dogs or cats know that humans die, or rather, that they eventually will die. It is not even clear that they know that *they* will die. That does not mean that they do not have a fear of death when it is at hand, or suspected. It is just that they probably don't spend any time at all thinking about it in advance. The way I do.

As I have been writing, it has struck me that I am trying to sound like an expert in these topics, whereas in fact there are no experts. It is as if someone were to tell you that women are more likely to save a human from a burning building than a man. Or that people, by and large, don't care what happens to other people in a disaster, only themselves (cats). You would correctly object: wait a minute, what an absurd generalization. Just because *you* have not witnessed this personally, you think it does not happen? Are you not aware that every person is different from every other person, and what one does is very different from what another does? Some people will risk their lives to save total strangers from drowning or from fire, or some other danger, while others will not.

All of us only know a small proportion of *all* humans, and no matter how well read, we are still limited in our knowledge. When you take a larger historical view, you realize that what we firmly believed some fifty years ago, is no longer true. As has been widely discussed, it was not long ago that it was considered easy to compile a list of qualities that were unique to humans: tool use, cultural transmission, language, emotional complexity, empathy, the ability to deceive, appreciation of art (aesthetic taste), architecture, and so on. One by one these so-called exclusively human abilities have fallen to more careful observation or research. It is even possible that some animals have a religious sense. So I am mindful that when I say cats don't do this, or dogs don't do that, I am speaking from a very limited perspective. Take my words not as gospel or as scientific certitude, but simply as a means of engaging discussion.

I say this not only with respect to abilities, but also in full awareness that each and every cat, and each and every dog, is unique in personality, every bit as much as humans are. But it is, I confess, difficult to always bear this in mind. So this morning a woman came with her nine-year-old son to see my pediatrician wife, and they brought their thirteen-week-old puppy. He was in a carrying case, and I knew, with certainty, that the minute they let him out, he would lick my hand and furiously wag his tail and look absolutely thrilled to see me and everyone else who came to have a look at him. Some infants might be like this, but many are not. However, I am sure I am not going out on a limb here to say that virtually *all* thirteen-week-old puppies will behave very much like this one: they are *designed* to show joy and win us over completely. All of them. True, they develop into very different dogs, depending on their later circumstances, but as puppies they all have that completely irresistible *joie de vivre*. (Older dogs have it, too, but no other animal, in my limited experience, has it to the extent that a puppy does—just about every puppy I have ever met, and I have met many.) Truth is, this is something of a mystery of evolution. Of course, I am aware of the theory that *all* baby animals are adorable, the better to make certain their parents enjoy being around them and want to take care of them. But I wonder if it is not just humans who find puppies this way, but whether other animals do as well? Sometimes of course the young are targeted by predators, so it could not be universally true. But what I have heard about elephants makes it seem likely that they respond to small, helpless, cute baby animals with something akin to pleasure, or in any event, without aggression.

Kittens are adorable, too, but in a different way. They are adorable, especially, when they are playing with one another, but they do not respond to humans with the same joyful abandon that puppies do. Already as kittens they are more self contained, more willing to go it alone.

If you do not respond to a puppy the puppy is caught off guard. She is perplexed. She is uncertain, as if to say, "what can this possibly mean?" She fully expects you to play with her and she is rarely rebuffed.

I believe that the above paragraphs help to explain why we are so hopelessly in love with dogs and cats: their whole life, from beginning to end, is designed to make us adore them. (Dogs, we have very recently learned, have even evolved a way of using their eyebrows to elicit our concern—maybe soon we will discover something similar in cats.) From day one they bring us joy in nearly un-diluted form. To lose this unique experience with their death comes as a shock. When we lose beloved humans we can look back at a life of ambivalence. Not so with dogs and cats. What could we possibly accuse them of?

The question that is perhaps foremost on most people's minds (at least those of us who think about these things) is whether people who love cats are as bereft when they die, as are the people who love dogs? The answer is clearly "yes," and you just need to go briefly on the internet to find examples that will convince even the most cat-proof skeptic that we bond with cats in very deep ways and mourn them equally deeply when they die. In fact, some people claim that the mourning process is even more in-tense for the simple reason that we usually live longer with a cat than with a dog because cats live, on aver-age, longer lives than dogs. It is not unusual for someone to spend twenty years with a cat. People often speak of "lonely old women, whose only companion is a cat" as if there was something pathological about being old, or a woman, or living with a cat. These are deep bonds, and it is never right to question them or in any way mock or belittle them. Remember, these two individuals can be to-gether night and day for a very long time. That makes for serious feelings. When a cat dies after this intimacy, it can be truly life altering. If such a woman is your friend, be there for her and let her tell you stories about her cat. They can be fascinating. Do not judge her. You will simply come off as a jerk.

What is it we miss in a cat? Well, for one, they are al-ways there. And it is the rare cat who does not greet you when you come into your house or your apartment, with the equivalent of "hi, where have you been? It's about time you're home." And of course, it never ceases to amaze us that this basically wild creature is inhabiting our home. What an honor. And so we miss that sense of having been singled out to share such a life, and also the sheer elegance of this animal who has such a light touch (used, as they are, to slinking through the jungle unseen and unheard). They lie on our laps, and when we are lucky, they even sleep with us. There can be few pleasures more intense than sleeping with a cat. Their bodies elongate to stretch out along ours, and then comes the magic, healing purr-ing, and then off to sleep, knowing that a completely wild animal trusts you enough to fall asleep in your arms. How can such a thing not be missed, and intensely so? There is only one remedy for the loss of a cat, and that is to eventually (and I am aware that this might be a long time) take yourself down to the nearest shelter and find another cat who needs you as much as you need her. Once you have lived with a cat, it is very hard to live without one. I should know: I have lived with dozens of cats in my seventy-nine years, and now that we are living in Sydney, and needing to move around a great deal, I discovered that I cannot have a cat in my life. It hurts. I am looking for a creative solution: perhaps a "shared" cat. In Spain I satisfied my desire to be around cats by visiting the wild cat colony on the beach every day, but I missed the intimacy that comes from sleeping with a cat. Few pleasures in life rival that experience.

Something I have learned from thinking about cats and death is just how little we know about death in other animals (some would say we don't know much about our own deaths either). Animals may have a better sense of it than we have thought possible. Living with cats and thinking about them has taught me just how ignorant we are of their different kinds of knowledge. Obviously, Oscar the cat knew something that nobody else did or even could. Was Oscar unique, or are cats just guarding their secrets? In any event, we need to pay careful attention to these mini tigers who deign to grace our lives with theirs.

5

∞

The Time of Death

Your pet doesn't know what we are doing or
why—they only know that you are there, that you
said it's ok, that you love them.

—A VETERINARIAN

I have to say that in general I am not a great fan of euthanasia. I guess what I mean by "in general" is for humans.
The reasons are not all that complicated: I have read widely
in the field of the killing of mental patients by the Third
Reich during World War II. It is not a pretty topic. I have
also begun reading about the current debates over euthanasia in Holland, Belgium, and the United States. I did
not like what I saw there, in particular in Belgium, where
there is a movement to allow euthanasia for depressed
children. I could hardly believe this so I read in greater
depth, and the more I read the more appalled I became.
An article in *The New Yorker* by Rachel Aviv (June 22,

2015)* reports on the controversial work of Dr. Wim Distelmans, a physician who is an enthusiastic advocate for euthanasia in very dubious cases, including children with so-called terminal depression—that is depression "resistant to treatment."†

Imagine if every time we had an illness that was resistant to treatment we were candidates for euthanasia! The point is, Distelmans is also the cochairman of the government certifying board, the Federal Euthanasia Commission, which decides when euthanasia is called for and when it is not. This commission has not yet decided against euthanasia in a single case. Given that Distelmans also runs an institute that provides euthanasia, this is at the very least a conflict of interest. He was broadly, I am glad to say, criticized just about everywhere for taking a group of psychiatrists to Auschwitz to "contemplate" euthanasia. Surely the Nazi center for killing people who, in the eyes of the Nazis, led "lives not worth living" is a stark reminder of the horrors of eugenic murder. But for Distelmans, who took seventy "health professionals"—doctors, psychologists, and nurses, all interested in euthanasia—to the camp in 2013, it was "an inspiring venue for organizing a seminar and reflecting on these issues so that we can consider and clarify confusions." Including of course the

---

* "The Death Treatment," *New Yorker,* https://www.newyorker.com/magazine/2015/06/22/the-death-treatment.

† Such cases are rare, but that they exist *at all* is reason for concern.

confusion of just exactly what he was doing on this tour to the world's most macabre site.

Fortunately this is not a topic we need to consider when it comes to our beloved animals (but I raised it as a matter of caution). At least I have never heard of anyone considering euthanasia for a dog or cat because the animal was depressed. So no, you do not put your dog or cat down because they appear depressed. You try to figure out what is making them sad and take that something away. But making dogs happy is so easy I will hardly address it—all you have to do is *be* with them. (Whether dogs should be on anti-depressants is a topic too far removed from the subject of this book for me to get into. Suffice it to say I am not in favor of drugs for dogs, cats, or humans. Diet, supplements, exercise, are all better options for us and for them. I realize this is not the standard view but I am very wary of all psychiatric drugs, primarily because of the side effects, which can be devastating.)

However there may well come a time when you feel that the end is approaching. It is nice to think that that time will hardly announce itself, that it will slip in one day and your dog will go to sleep right next to you as usual, but when you wake up, the dog or cat will not be breathing anymore. That could, in theory, happen, but it does so rarely. Far more frequently there is a slow decline. You pick up the leash that means walk and, instead of racing to the door and doing his little happiness dance, he just looks up at you with sad eyes. "Not today, but thanks for thinking of me." And then it dawns on you that he is not lazy or stubborn; he is in pain. He's not a whiner, so he doesn't make a big fuss, but you know that his physical strength is beginning to go. Sometimes this is a very slow process and you are able to witness every small change, but at other times it seems to come out of the blue. The dog you have always known is suddenly a different dog. Or rather the same dog, but with limitations you never even knew existed.

So what do you do when you are not in a hurry for a final visit to your vet? You engage in my favorite medical term, *watchful waiting*. Even if you know it is terminal, you wait. This period can be long and satisfying for both of you: lots of cuddling, lots of exclamations of love, lots of together time. Long winter evenings curled up in bed, her eyes always fixed on you. Not able to go outdoors any longer—her world has shrunk. You are it. You have suddenly become her all. She doesn't complain, she compensates, and this compensation takes the form of adoration. She adores you. Not because she suddenly needs you, but because that is her nature. That is how she is made, but under these changed circumstances you are able to perceive it more easily or, let us say, it is manifest in an even purer form. For some people, and surely for many dogs, this is the high point of their relationship, the one that comes shortly before it must end. There is a moving video of a young man and his dog who both develop cancer at the same time, and how they supported each other with love, a unique and different kind of love than they were getting from anyone else. From the over one thousand comments (nearly two million people have watched the seven-minute video) you can see how touched everyone was by this story. Hardly anyone could stop themselves from crying.*

Will your animal let you know when it is time to let go? Not always. They are holding on to you as much as you are holding on to them. They don't want you to leave them any more than you want them to leave you. So how do we know then when the time has come? The honest answer is that we don't know. But here is the important part: neither does anyone else. So taking your dog to a vet, especially to one you may not know well, may not be the solution, as the answer you receive could be incorrect. There are of course clues, and all of us have our own red-lines: for example, what if the dog is incontinent? I would have to say this is just not a redline. I say this from direct and immediate experience: as I have mentioned earlier, our son Ilan is in Berlin, even as I write these lines. He is living with Benjy, our beloved yellow Lab about whom I wrote *The Dog Who Couldn't Stop Loving*. Benjy still goes for two-hour walks with Ilan through the Berlin parks, and

---

* https://www.youtube.com/watch?v=P2zQbsEGh_Q.

the colder the weather the happier he is. But he has begun to be incontinent. And not just in the house. Since he
sleeps with Ilan, and always has since both were young,
Ilan wakes up some days to find the bed soiled. Not fun,
I agree. But neither for me nor for Ilan is this a sign of the
end. It can be cleaned up. Dog diapers will be tried. Rub-
ber mats, plastic, a large dog bed that is easy to clean on
top of the human bed. Nothing more than a problem to be
solved (and a first sign, true). So, yes, it is true that Benjy is
slowly reaching the point where he is no longer the dog he
once was, except when it comes to loving. He has bursts
of speed still, especially in a new park, but mostly he has
slowed down considerably. Ilan doesn't know if it is painful for Benjy to walk or if he just does not have the strength.
He does go out every day at least three times, and he en-
joys being outside, but the change is obvious. He is now a
very old dog for a big golden Labrador retriever. It is extremely painful for Ilan to go through this process and he
turns to me for guidance: "Dad, how will I know that the
time has come? And I am letting you know in advance,
Dad, that you and Mom will have to come at a moment's
notice from Australia to be with me when I have to take
him for the last time to the vet. I cannot do it by myself."
He is right. But it will be no easier for me or for Leila. I
have never been present for such a thing with any of my
many animals, and I am not sure how I will react. Puppy
died in my arms; Taffy ate poison; Misha died quietly in

his sleep. I was in Berkeley when my father died in Los Angeles. I was in Australia when my mother died in New Zealand. With the exception of Puppy, I have not been present for a single death in all my seventy-nine years. Odd. I can't say I am eager to witness the last moment of a beloved companion. It must be a strange feeling. I know that some people describe it as peaceful, and they are glad they were there, and of course your friend wants you to be there (I am thinking of the vet who said that dogs look around for their companion in their last moment). I just find the prospect of being present for the very last moment of your friend's life overwhelming.

Even if you agree with me that losing control of the bowels is not all that serious, what happens when the signs point to something that is in fact more serious? Not eating? In obvious pain? No longer drinking? Unable to get up? Unable to walk? Much more serious, I agree. But my hope at this moment (coming in the next year or two for sure) is that I will not have to take a unilateral step. Benjy cannot look at me and say it is time, nor can I trust myself enough to interpret his look to mean that. So I am hoping that he will simply not wake up one morning. Ilan will wake up, but Benjy will not. Ilan will be inconsolable, but he will have been spared both the prospect of Benjy's suffering *and* making the decision himself to give Benjy a final injection. I know that many of my readers will find giving Benjy a final injection the kindest solution, and perhaps it is the bravest, but I have to say that I cannot quite imagine it for myself. I just do not see myself putting Benjy's head into my lap, watch him look up at me with complete trust, and then nod to the vet to go ahead and give him the final injection. I just don't see how I can stand it. It is not for me like a dear relative who has begged you to do just that. He is a dog who cannot consent. The decision must be mine and I just cannot be sure what he would say if he could. Maybe, yes, he would say the time had come. But maybe, too, he would beg me to wait just one more day, or one more week. Maybe he, too, envisages simply not waking up and would, just like me, much prefer that. I am just a little bit uncomfortable with how easy it seems to some to take a dog or cat for a final vet visit. I say some, because I realize that for most people this is one of the most difficult decisions of their life. There are times when it is selfish to do it and others when it is selfish not to do it. If only one could discuss it with the animal. They obviously have the answer but cannot give it to us. (Some people tell me that their animal does let them know that the time has come.) But for me the problem is that we can never be certain that the right decision has been made and has been made at the right time. It is hard to get help on this, almost as if that is the burden we take on when we bring an animal into our house. But I see no harm in asking people who are close to your animal what they think. Ultimately, though, you have to make the decision alone. Once it is clear that physical suffering is intense and cannot be improved and all other avenues are closed off, then it is time for that terrible visit to the vet. But I do sometimes worry that it can come too soon. One reason I hesitate to advocate for euthanasia (except of course when the physical agony becomes unbearable for your animal, even though this is difficult and sometimes impossible to establish) is my experience with my mother.

My mother had severe dementia. She lived to ninety-seven and died in exactly the way I hope for Benjy. She closed her eyes and did not open them again. Once, some years before, when I saw the ravage of her dementia, I asked her if she wished she could die. She looked completely shocked. "Absolutely not!" was her vigorous reply. And in truth, while I found the quality of her life sorely lacking, I am not sure she did. She was happy almost all of the time, still laughing frequently at her own jokes and smiling a good deal. She was not suffering, even if I was. She could barely walk. She took little food. But I could not enter into her mind to judge the quality of her life. I would never have allowed a doctor to end her life. Maybe I would have had a different reaction if I had known she was suffering unbearable pain. And that is true also for animals: intractable pain is not something one wishes on anyone, human or other.

I am hoping for something similar for Benjy. But if you disagree with me, I can only urge you to at least consider making the final moments at home, where your dog or cat is most comfortable, and not in a cold office and, above all, not with a veterinarian they do not know. I am not a great one for human rituals (even if I have been persuaded by my editor to add a chapter about it for animals), but here I would urge you to make the last day one filled with rituals that your dog will understand: his or her favorite toys, favorite place, lots of stroking and love talk, treats, people dropping in to say good-bye. Even other animals who have been friends. Or you may feel it is too hard on the animal to be forced to interact with others—that perhaps she should be surrounded only by immediate family. But no matter how wonderful those moments are, the one moment you are dreading will come. I cannot tell you how to get through that, because I don't really know. If it is any consolation, and it should be, your dog or cat will not feel any pain. Nonetheless I dread seeing Benjy's eyes as he looks at me for the last time, perhaps comprehending that this is it and he will not see me again. But in all likelihood, he will not think that. More likely he will think he is just going to sleep and that when he wakes up he will be in my bed again and I will be there, and he will lick my face as he always does and we will be together. I wish I could think that, too.

A friend, Jean Frances, sent me this account of the loss of her two kittens. I found the dream especially remarkable.

I adopted Kitty when a friend of a friend died of cancer. When Kitty was about fifteen years old he had problems with his kidneys. After about a week of intensive inpatient treatment, they told me Kitty was not responding. I did not want to give up, so they trained me to continue the treatments at home, which included subcutaneous infusions of special fluids. That first night was a struggle for us both. Kitty used to sleep in my bed, but when he tried to get up he was unable to do so. I wanted to pull him up, but I was afraid that he would not be able to get up and down again if he needed to go to the bathroom or something. I had fixed a bed for him in the kitchen that was near his food and not far from his box. As he walked away, I heard what I now know to have been a death rattle. Early the next morning, I went into the kitchen and Kitty appeared to be resting, but then he started having convulsions and I sensed he was about to die. I did not know what to do because the vet was not even open yet. Then, in front of my very eyes, Kitty shook, and with a loud yowl, he gave up the spirit. I felt so helpless. I just stood there paralyzed and watched him die. I promised myself I would not subject my other cat, Sweetie Pie to a prolonged ordeal when her time came. I felt that, because I had not been able to accept the inevitability of Kitty's death, I had allowed him to go through unnecessary and extended trauma. Sweetie Pie continued to live a long and fluffy life. But, when she was nineteen, her health, too, began to fail. She lost a lot of weight, suffered from thyroid problems, glaucoma and chronic eye infection, and became incontinent. None of the medical treatments seemed to be working and she continued to lose weight. A number of friends thought I should help her die, but I did not want to. One friend advised me not to put my own needs in front of Sweetie Pie's. Another thought that Sweetie Pie's dignity was at stake because of her incontinence and that she would want to die, but I had trouble seeing it that way. Not knowing what to do, I prayed for wisdom and clarity to know what was right.

The next night I had a dream which was odd but illuminating. I dreamed that I took Sweetie Pie to church for a blessing but ended up leaving her there for final disposition. After I left, I felt terrible and went back to the church because I had not had a chance to truly say good-bye. When I got there, they told me Sweetie Pie had already been taken to another place for the final act. I went to the place in a hurry, hoping I would get there in time. Strangely, the place was not a regular vet, but also served as an auto wrecking yard. I begged to see her, fearing she was already gone. But she was still alive, and they brought her out to me. I wanted to hold her in my arms and tell her that I was going to end her life for her sake so that she could avoid suffering. But when I looked in her face, she was so happy to see me, because she thought I had come to save her. I could not bear to say those words to her under the circumstances, and then I woke up, calling out her name. She was lying at the foot of my bed and meowed sweetly in response. I was so happy and knew for certain that her time had not come.

Over the next two months Sweetie Pie's health continued to decline. I took her for more tests and tried a new vet for a second opinion, but unfortunately the news was not encouraging. I was told that to die naturally would be painful for Sweetie Pie, but I had trouble knowing when I should just give up and set the appointment. The new vet decided to try yet another intervention, but it would take a few weeks to see if it was successful. I set a provisional appointment for euthanasia, but with the hope that if Sweetie Pie rallied it could be converted to a regular checkup.

About a week later I woke up and saw Sweetie Pie lying at my side. She tried to get up but couldn't. She did not have the strength. I looked at her and I knew. My cat was not sick. She was dying. I carried her to the kitchen for some food and water and she had a little bit, and then I had to carry her back. I called and made an appointment for the very next day. When I awoke that morning, I carried her once more to the kitchen and sat her in front of her water bowl, but this time, she could not even hold her head up. She started leaning forward into the bowl. Fortunately, the appointment was in about an hour, and the friend who used to care for her when I was out of town went to the vet with us. It was raining and I wrapped Sweetie Pie in a brand-new towel and carried her in. The vet was very compassionate and allowed me to hold her through the entire process. Sweetie Pie's last memories were hugs and kisses.

I had a special box prepared for her with a fresh towel and a rose. We returned to my home and buried her next to my house, and now there is a rose bush growing in that place.

This story illustrates how confounding, confusing, and agonizing it is for us to be in charge of making the final decision. Veterinarians are of course the authorities here, but I fear that some of them, being so close to death, and being constantly involved in administering euthanasia, might not always be as sensitive to the fact that the animal in front of them has been deeply loved and will be deeply missed, and no decision is more important than the one about to be made. There is never a good time for an animal friend to die. But some times are better than others. If only we could be certain that we have recognized that moment.

I still believe that the most important thing for your animal at the end is for you to be there if you possibly can. Having said that, and believing it, I need a word of explanation of how it is that Benjy is now living in Berlin, and we are living in Sydney, Australia. When we took Benjy with us to Berlin two years ago, we thought we were moving there permanently. As things turned out, however, we had to return after a year to Australia. Naturally we wanted to bring Benjy back with us so we could all be together. But our vet in Berlin explained that at his age, a long trip of nearly forty hours, could well prove fatal. He could not, in all good conscience, give us a certificate that would permit the trip. Moreover, even if Benjy could travel, once in Australia he would need to be in quarantine in a different city, Melbourne, for some weeks. We agreed that he probably would not survive all of this. As I have explained, he is not with a stranger. On the contrary, he is with his best friend, our son Ilan who has known him his entire life. They are happy to be together even if Benjy is no longer the dog he once was. Leila and I plan to travel to Berlin at some point this year (2019) to say our final good-byes. It will not be easy. It is never easy for anyone to say good-bye to their beloved animals. I have become fully conscious of this in writing this book.

6

∞

Grieving the Wild Friend

Grief is the price we all pay for love.

—COLIN MURRAY PARKES

What about the death of an animal who is not domesticated? How does that compare to the death of dogs and cats and birds who have been living with humans, as companions, for thousands of generations?

The basic question is whether we can really become friends with a wild animal. Not so long ago there would have been widespread skepticism about this possibility. But, thanks to the internet, we have access to stories from around the world that have remained, until now, mostly hidden. We know that people have managed to enter into some kind of relationship with an animal that is decidedly not domesticated, in fact completely wild. But there is a caveat: most of these animals are indeed from wild species, but for some reason or another, they have had long or intense relations with a human.

Sanctuaries are extraordinary places where much of the philosophical points I want to make in this chapter can be researched in visible terms. What I mean is that a lot of animals who wind up at sanctuaries, are, or were, wild. Sometimes they were wild by nature, and sometimes they were truly not domesticated. But something quite unusual happens at a sanctuary, and I have seen this many times, at all the inspiring sanctuaries I have visited. The animals come to know that they are safe; that they will not be abused (I wonder, too, if they realize they will not be killed); and that the people at the sanctuaries are their friends. One sanctuary in particular has been very dear to me: Animal Place in the foothills of the Sierra Nevada in Northern California. It was founded by the indomitable Kim Sturla. When I was there last, I was particularly impressed with the turkeys who lived there. I had no idea just how affectionate they could become, and how it was possible to form a deep attachment to them. Here is what Kim wrote me:

In turkey land, male turkeys, better looking than the gals, are the ones who usually strut their stuff. But Tracey was the most beautiful female turkey I had ever seen. All white, with extraordinarily long tail feathers, she paraded the garden like a stunning swan gliding over a pond. Typical of the adolescent glamour girls I remember from my youth, she was a bitch. She would peck Ellie's head for no apparent reason, seemingly just to remind Ellie of the pecking order, ravishing beauties at the top.

Ellie was nondescript. She was small with short tail feathers, probably extra short thanks to Tracey's pecking and plucking. But Ellie was the sweetest turkey I had ever met. Anybody who has spent time at a sanctuary, where turkeys are treated lovingly and respond in kind, knows that is saying a lot. You couldn't pet Ellie while she was eating because she would lose all interest in food in favor of affection, and big Tracey would end up with double. As I would usher my turkey girls towards their sleeping crate in the evening, Ellie would often just plop down on the grass like an immovable boulder, until she'd had a few minutes of stroking and tickling under the wing, in that same side of the lower back area where dogs love to be scratched, "the spot."

For years I have had a recurring nightmare, which I hear is common among animal advocates: I am out doing something and then realize I have forgotten my dogs. I left them somewhere a full day ago, locked without food and water, and I wonder if they have died because of my neglect. A few months ago, I got truly worried I might enact that dream with my turkeys. I had moved into a new home where the girls were not in front of my window as I worked, to beg to be let out of their coop, or to demand breakfast and dinner. I was finding my workload overwhelming. Often at my desk in the early morning before it was safe to let the turkeys out of their coyote proof sleeping crate, I occasionally forgot them for hours.

One busy morning I remembered them at 11 AM and realized I had better set myself alarms. I set their up-and-at-'em alarm for 8 AM, once coyotes cleared the neighborhood, and their dinner alarm for 4:30 PM. The dogs worked as their bedtime alarm, urging me every sunset to head out for a walk on the bluff. On the way back we would walk through the turkey yard, and I would put the girls to bed.

This morning, as I pieced together the evening before, I realized I had been writing hard when sunset came, so my housemates took the dogs to the bluff. I was working on a piece for the *Los Angeles Times* about a French bulldog who was killed when he was put in a United Airlines overhead bin.

I called it a day long after dark, made a quick dinner, plopped down for my nightly dose of Netflix, and went to bed. And my worst nightmare came true.

"Don't go out there," Clive said this morning,

with stern and kind concern. But I am not the type to avoid the body of a beloved. I walked into a garden strewn with feathers, and whole egg yolks, long lines of intestine, and an organ that appeared to be a liver.

I saw two carcasses together in the corner. One was less a carcass than a shell; Tracey had been emptied out and picked clean. But the forty or so pound coyote, surely overstuffed after eating twenty-five-pound Tracey, had hardly touched the meat on Ellie. She was headless though, and I am grateful for that, because I pray that the loss of a head was a quick death. And I am grateful that her head was nowhere to be found in the garden, because given how much I loved to kiss her little beak and feel her warm breath on my lips, I don't think I could have borne the sight of that little beak breathless.

On lighter work mornings, I would sit and cuddle the girls as I drank my coffee or meditated in our garden. Today I sat with their remains. As the sun rose, my sweethearts started to smell like the meat department at Whole Foods.

A good instinct told me to call Susie Coston, the manager at Farm Sanctuary. She adores turkeys, and would understand my pain. And I figured that having cared for thousands of animals over the years she was bound to know how it felt to be responsible for a death. She assured me that accidents happen, particularly when people are stressed and when they break their routines, as I had yesterday.

She also assured me that my girls' deaths would have been fast. Unlike humans, coyotes almost always make fast kills. As Tracey and Ellie had been saved from the slaughter industry, I thought of their sisters who had been trucked to slaughterhouses, then strung upside-down in shackles on conveyor belts.

Susie suggested I shouldn't feel the need to share what had happened: "You know how people are." Indeed. I thought of mothers who had left their babies in the bath to answer the phone, remembered them not in the nick of time, as many mothers have, but instead a minute too late, and then faced police charges rather than immense compassion on the worst day of their lives.

I know how people are because I am one of them. The night my turkeys died I was judging both the flight attendant who insisted, and the woman who relented when her dog was ordered into an overhead bin on a United flight. Now I share my pain in knowing how completely I betrayed two beings who depended on me. If I am judged harshly, perhaps I will learn compassion for those who are judged harshly when responsible for stupidity that leads to tragedy.

I know not everybody will see turkey death as tragedy. For most people it's lunch. But I think we have come to a time when many readers will understand my heartbreak. People are starting to realize that the distinctions we make between animals we pet and animals we eat are arbitrary, which is why they differ between countries. Grief is grief, and whether it be for a French bulldog in a carrier case, or two beloved mangled turkeys in a garden, the guilt and sorrow are the same.

I am not sure if these turkeys were wild or domesticated, or if it makes any difference to the grief that Kim felt. But sometimes the animal is indeed wild, so wild that they cannot be kept in human surrounds. This is the case with Christian the lion. Christian the lion was a lion born in captivity and purchased in 1969 by Australians John Rendall and Anthony "Ace" Bourke from Harrods department store in London. For the first year, life was fun for all three of them. But when the lion turned one, it became clear that the big city was no place for a large, fully grown lion. When Bill Travers and Virginia McKenna, stars of the film *Born Free,* visited Rendall and Bourke and met Christian, they suggested that Bourke and Rendall ask the assistance of George Adamson. Adamson, a Kenyan conservationist, who together with his wife Joy raised and released Elsa the lioness, agreed to reintegrate Christian into the wild at their compound in the Kora National Reserve in Kenya. One year after Adamson released Christian to the wild, Ace and John decided they would travel to Africa, in the perhaps vain hope that they could find Christian. If they did, would he remember them, or attack them? They had heard that he was now the head of a pride of lions, and there was always a risk. They set out to search the jungle, hoping to find their friend. They succeeded. The YouTube video of the encounter, has been viewed more than sixty million times.* I am friends with Ace Bourke, and I understand why this single encounter has stamped his life forever. In the video you see Christian with his pride. He sees the men, and slowly ambles toward them, almost like a cat about to catch an unsuspecting bird. Then he starts racing toward them. Ace told me his heart was racing, too. He was either about to have the most intense meeting of his life, or he would be mauled to death by a large adult lion who was once his friend. Christian rushes up, stands on his hind legs and hugs the two men like they were his long lost brothers. You see him lick them all over their faces, going from one to the other, clearly ecstatic to see his old friends again. And then, astonishingly, his pride walks up to the men, and rub up against their legs

---

* http://www.alioncalledchristian.com.au/.

just as your house cat does. The men reach down and pet a completely wild lion whom they have never seen before, nor has the lion seen them. Adamson keeps a discrete distance. He is not sure how he, a stranger, will be accepted. He need not have worried. Friends of friends are welcome. It is hard to watch this clip without being enchanted. We do not expect a large wild cat to remain attached to a member of another species and show joy at seeing them again. I guess, too, it tells us something of what the natural world would be like if all humans treated other animals as friends rather than as food or enemies.

A step further are people who rescue a wild animal, and the animal, in what to all intents and purposes appears to show gratitude, stays in touch with that human, or even decides to live together with their savior.

Such was the case with Pocho the crocodile, and the man who saved his life, Chito, a poor fisherman from Siquirres, Costa Rica. In 1989 Chito found a crocodile lying on the bank of the Reventazón River. He had been shot in the head through his left eye. He was alone and helpless. He was a large crocodile, yet he weighed no more than 150 pounds. He was slowly dying. Chito decided he could not simply walk away from the poor animal. He carried him to his boat and brought him home. For the next six months he slept next to the suffering animal, feeding him as he slowly regained his strength. He said later: "Food wasn't enough. The crocodile needed my love to regain the will to live," His wife was appalled and told him it was her or Pocho. He chose Pocho. Eventually, after three years of patience, Pocho was healed, and had regained his 1,000-pound weight (he was sixteen feet long), and was well enough to return to the wild. Reluctantly Chito took him to a nearby river and released him with a final farewell. Chito returned home, and went to sleep. But when he woke the next morning, there was Pocho, sleeping peacefully on his veranda. From then on, the two became inseparable. They would swim together, and even though when Chito would first jump into the lake, Pocho would swim toward him with his mouth open and his teeth bared, as he got closer and saw who it was, he would close his jaws and wait for the kiss that Chito always gave him. For the next twenty years they stayed together, swimming and performing "their act" for tourists. Pocho died of natural causes in 2011 and was given a state funeral.*

It is entirely remarkable, as a friendship between a crocodile and a human had never before been observed. It was thought to be simply impossible. Crocodiles are one of the few animals who regard humans as food. Roger Horrocks, a South African filmmaker who shot a fine documentary about Pocho and Chito had an experience

---

* You can see footage of the two swimming together here: https://www .youtube.com/watch?v=I7fZZUfvx0s.

in South Africa where he was cave diving when he and
a companion found themselves inside a cave face to face
with a large crocodile. The crocodile seemed amused by
their presence and tolerated them as they took footage of
the animal who almost appears to be smiling. Horrocks
began to wonder, then, whether it would be possible to
"tame" a wild crocodile. That is how he heard of Pocho
and Chito and traveled to Costa Rica to film them together.
He does a good job of expressing his shock and astonishment at what he saw. Chito would go out at night, during the full moon, and slip into the water and call Pocho.
Horrocks is horrified: crocodiles are famous for being
at their most aggressive during the night. This is when
they hunt. How could anyone ever cross the barrier that
separates one of nature's most perfect predators with the
helpless prey-animal that is the unarmed human? Yet his
film demonstrates that this actually happened, and that
an intimacy developed between the two species that is,
in theory, impossible. Yes, humans could develop a lik-
ing for crocodiles and maybe even fool themselves into
thinking it was a kind of love. But how could they fool
themselves enough to believe it could possibly be reciprocated by a giant reptilian apex predator? At the end of
this unusual documentary, called *The Man Who Swims
with Crocodiles,* Horrocks wants to enter the water with
Pocho on his own to see what would happen. It almost
ended very badly: the body language of the giant croc

was not reassuring, and it was clear that the relationship he had with Chito did not include other humans. When Pocho died, Chito was disconsolate. Of course. He felt he had truly loved and that the love was reciprocated. It was indeed a unique relationship and does raise the question of whether the love was based on familiarity or was due to some other extraneous cause: what Horrocks hypothesizes is that because Pocho had been found by Chito on the point of death, perhaps some part of his brain that would ordinarily incline him to aggression, had been altered.

Horrocks notes, and I have heard this, too, that many people who believe they have been befriended by a wild predator, are rudely awakened to find the animal attacking them, and sometimes killing them, even when they have been together for years. Would you swim with a shark, even if he appeared to have no animosity toward humans? I wouldn't.

Many people, unfortunately, regard fish as animals with whom it is impossible to form any kind of relationship, let alone an intimate one. I can remember, when I was doing the research for my book *When Elephants Weep,* meeting a very distinguished professor of biology at UC Berkeley who specialized in fish. He was immensely knowledgeable about every variety of fish imaginable. He had many fish in small aquariums. I asked if he thought that perhaps the fish became bored in such tiny quarters.

He blew up at me for even suggesting that fish could have such feelings, or any feelings for that matter. That was some years ago, and I like to think that the good professor will have changed his mind, especially in light of an influential and wonderful book by Jonathan Balcombe called *What a Fish Knows,* the gist of which is that fish are extraordinarily diverse and complex, with mental, social, and emotional capacities that put them on par with birds and mammals.*

In that book he tells a remarkable story, and I reached out to the woman who told it to him, Tali Ovadia, and asked her to give me more details. Here is what she wrote me:

Three years ago I went to the pet store to get a pufferfish. I already had a community tank of other fish and knew puffers needed to be alone so [I] got a twelve gallon tank and my first puffer, a tiny Fahaka freshwater creature who looked more like a Seuss character than anything else. What drew me to him was his cartoon face and the way he held my gaze when I stared into his near iridescent eyes. I was hooked, and thus began my relationship with Mango.

---

* For more about this, the author summarizes his book in *The Globe & Mail,* under "Fish Are Not Office Decorations": https://www.theglobeandmail.com /opinion/article-fish-are-not-office-decorations/.

Over the years my fascinating little fish and I developed an unexpected bond that had me leaving parties early to feed him on time, asking my neighbor to "spend time with him" when I was out of town, and generally thinking about him far more than I'm willing to say. Essentially, I loved this fish as much as I'd ever loved anything else.

Coming home was predictably joyous as Mango would always madly swim to the front of his tank and wag his body as I'd walk through the door. Every day we'd stare at each other for extended time and yes, communicate. "I see you" was the general sentiment. "I appreciate you." I swear he'd smile at me.

Eleven years passed and Mango and I had our routines like any relationship. I was very diligent about his care and never considered a life without him, until the day I came home, and he didn't swim to me, which had never happened. I knew it was the beginning of the end and had a vet come to see if there was anything I could do for him. She said he'd already outlived the average lifespan and likely had cancer. I was crushed. Over the next 10 days I watched my little sentient struggle and fade until his time here was complete. I cried a tankful of tears and buried him in the backyard with the jade buddha that lived in his tank with him.

I'm still in awe over the connection and depth I experienced with my little fish and miss Mango every day.

I maintain that we have absolutely no right to doubt Tali's account of her own feelings. Some of you may be inclined to doubt those of the fish. I am not, but I do agree that the feelings of an animal in captivity, no matter how benign, are not exact mirrors to feelings of a completely wild animal. And that is why I found this account by the late Val Plumwood so enthralling. Val Plumwood was an Australian ecofeminist philosopher who died in 2008. She is perhaps best known for an incident that made her world famous but which she no doubt would rather not have happened: I have told this story in a previous book (*Beasts*) but here is a brief summary:

During a visit to the magnificent Kakadu National Park (the setting of *Crocodile Dundee,* filmed there a few months after the attack), near Darwin in Australia, Plumwood had camped at the East Alligator ranger station and borrowed a four-meter-long, fiberglass canoe from the park ranger, to explore the East Alligator River (the name alone should have alerted her, even if she called it Alligator Lagoon).

When I pulled my canoe over in driving rain to a rock outcrop rising out of the swamp for a hasty, sodden lunch, I experienced the unfamiliar sensation of being watched. I had not gone more than five or ten minutes back down the channel when, rounding a bend, I saw ahead of me in midstream what looked like a floating stick—one I did not recall passing on my way up. As the current moved me toward it, the stick appeared to develop eyes.

Plumwood grabbed some overhanging branches, but before she could pull herself up, the crocodile seized her between the legs and dragged her under the water, a "centrifuge of whirling, boiling blackness, which seemed about to tear my limbs from my body, driving waters into my bursting lungs."

The crocodile briefly let her go, then seized her again, subjecting her to three such "death rolls" before she managed to escape up a steep mud bank. Despite severe injuries—her left leg was exposed to the bone, she crawled the three kilometers to the ranger station. She spent a month in intensive care in a hospital in Darwin, followed by extensive skin grafts. Later, upon reflection, she came up with this calm and deep insight:

As my own narrative and the larger story were ripped apart, I glimpsed a shockingly indifferent world in which I had no more significance than any other edible being. The thought, *This can't be hap-*

pening to me, I'm a human being. I am more than just food! was one component of my terminal incredulity. It was a shocking reduction, from a complex human being to a mere piece of meat. Reflection has persuaded me that not just humans, but any creature can make the same claim to be more than just food. We are edible, but we are also much more than edible.

And so when the ranger offered to find and kill the crocodile that had attacked her, she refused, claiming, rightly alas, that the crocodile was simply being himself. There was no malice involved, only hunger.

I am only telling this gruesome but instructive story as an introduction to Plumwood's extraordinary friendship with a completely wild animal found only in Australia, a wombat.

A wombat is an Australian marsupial that looks like a cross between a beaver and a badger. Tourists to Australia think they are giant rats. They would have to be some rat: wombats can be four feet long and weigh up to a hundred pounds. Because of their size, they have few predators. They can race away at speeds of up to twenty-five miles an hour, faster than Usain Bolt. They appear to have little fear of humans and we have seen them sitting peaceably by the side of the road when we were driving through rural Australia. When born they are the size of a pea, and they spend their entire first year inside their mother's pouch, and the next year inside the burrow with their mother right next to them. They have a very slow metabolism: it takes them fourteen days to digest their food, mostly kangaroo grass. They are considered, by Australians, as somewhat dim, but their cerebral hemispheres are proportionately larger than in any other marsupial. They adjust rather easily to captivity, quickly becoming housebroken, and will come when called by name. But the question is: Why would anyone want to enslave (capture) a wild animal? It has always seemed to me wrong. Here is what Val said about "her" wombat:

My wombat Birubi died after a brief illness sometime around Wednesday 18 August 1999. I miss Birubi greatly and continue to catch his beloved form (or "ghost") out of the corner of my eye, a half-seen image flitting around the corner of a cupboard or across the veranda. Long after his death, my eyes continued to search out his shape on the moonlit grass. He was part of my life for so long—over twelve years—that I found it hard to believe he would no longer wait for me or greet me, that he was finally gone.

Birubi came to me from the wildlife rescue service as a malnourished and very sick orphan. His mother had probably died of the mange, a disease introduced by Europeans with their dogs that bring so many wombats to an early and tormented death. Since my own human son had recently died, Birubi and I bonded strongly. Birubi (the name, meaning I believe "the drum," was given him by his first carers in the rescue service) was about a year old, furred but still suckling, when he took up residence with me. He seemed to have suffered greatly from his mother's death and was desperate for care.

Birubi had received from his wombat mother a good quality wombat education; she had taught him to defecate outside the burrow (or its equivalent, my house), and the rudiments of survival in the bush. Within a day of arriving he learnt to open the sliding glass doors of the house and could go outside into the bush whenever he wished (which was often). His ability to control the access between his world and mine enabled him to be active in choosing and structuring the balance between us, to enter my world while still fully retaining his wombatness. He was generally wary of humans until he had clearly established their identity, and would exit the house if it was too noisy or unsettling.

Once established in his own nearby burrows in the forest, he came to the house on a visiting basis on the average for an hour or so most evenings for personal, moral and material support. (At his behest I supplemented his grazing with carrots and rolled oats, which corresponded to the roots and seeds sections of the wombat diet). In the first year he would spend part of the night out of doors, and part in my bed with me.

I was always conscious of a dimension of mystery in my knowledge of Birubi's mind. The sense of bridging a great gulf of difference was part of the magic of the relationship. I think it was the centrality of the mother-child relationship to both our species.

Birubi, like other wombats and unlike dogs, was a resilient and determined animal who could not be shaped to human will. He did not recognize human superiority or pretensions to own the world and had a strong sense of his own independent selfhood, his own equal interests and entitlements. This stubbornness and sense of equality is the feature that has brought the wombat so strongly into conflict with the farmer, but to me it was wonderful. It meant that you were dealing with a real other; that contact had to be on his terms and not just on yours. Discipline, punishment and training to accept human will, of the sort we apply to dogs, were out of the question; not only would they be totally ineffective, but they would jeopardize the entire basis of our relationship.

I feel it was an incredible privilege to be allowed to know a free, wary and basically wild animal so intimately and richly. Our relationship cut across the usual boundary between the wild and domestic, the forest and the house, the non-human and the human, nature and culture.

It was enchanting, the enchantment of childhood imagination and story, to walk side by side with Birubi along a forest track, to look up from my desk to find a forest-dwelling wombat sitting in my armchair by the fire. You had the courage and freedom to cross the boundary, Birubi. But do we?

"*Ave atque vale,* [I salute you and Good-bye] Birubi. We will remember you."

So what was Val grieving? Whatever she tells us she was grieving for. That's the lesson we all need to take to heart: we have no business telling anyone that they are falsely grieving, that they have no right to grieve. It is only natural to grieve something that is so rare: not many people on earth have had close encounters with wombats and perhaps Val was grieving this or just the fact that it was such a mystery and was so wonderful while it was there, and now it is not there. I would imagine that this could apply broadly: the animal we loved was there, was with us, was aware of us, looked at us, felt something for us, and now that animal is gone, and will not be with us, will no longer look at us, or feel anything for us.

Let's pause for a moment to think about the difference between the two stories: The lessons that Val learned from the attack by the crocodile is that we are not the absolute top of the food chain after all, or that the very idea of a food chain is misleading. "I was suddenly transformed in the parallel universe into the form of a small, edible animal whose death was of no more significance than that of a mouse," she wrote.

We were just meat for the crocodile. As we probably are for some sharks. But we like the fantasy (or rather, some people like me do) of being able to interact even with large predators as if we were all one big happy family (even one big happy family is not always a happy family). So we are fascinated when somebody becomes buddy-buddy with a predator, like a crocodile, a shark, a grizzly bear, a large cat. But the fantasy, while sometimes shared by the animal in question, is often not shared, and we make a fatal mistake in thinking it is. Hippos, for example, are known to turn on their human "friend" and decapitate them with a single bite. Big cats also.

And bears. Bears perhaps more than just about any other animal, especially large Russian bears in Kamchatka. That brings to mind the late great Canadian Charlie Russell and his bears. Charlie Russell, who died in 2018 at the age of seventy-six, was a self-schooled expert on bears. And what an expert he was. Many regarded him as the single greatest authority on brown bears in the world. Russell spent twelve years living with grizzly bears on Russia's remote eastern Kamchatka Peninsula, studying their behavior and learning to live alongside them. Most people think of bears as solitary, bad-tempered, dangerous animals. They can be. But Charlie believed "that it's an intelligent, social animal that is completely misunderstood." To prove it, he would spend at least three months every year for ten years in a completely isolated dark forest in Kamchatka in a small cabin he built himself while slowly befriending the bears. The problem is that even in such a remote area as he chose, there were people who were interested in the bears for a different reason: they wanted their gall bladders, which are considered an aphrodisiac and medicine in certain parts of Asia, and are worth their weight in gold. When he returned to Kamchatka in 2003, all his bear-friends were gone. They had been slaughtered. A bear gall bladder was nailed to the door of his cabin, as a warning.

He had become interested in bears when his father, a noted naturalist, took him and his brother to Princess Royal Island in British Columbia, and the bears there ran from them. They went back to the base camp and left their guns behind. The bears seemed to understand that they were then not a threat, allowing them to come closer than before, and this gave Charlie the idea that bears were not as aggressive as people believed. They were only defending themselves.

Charlie told his father he didn't want to go to college to study bears, he wanted to go to the bears to learn about bears. They would be his teachers, not the object of his study. He wanted to be around bears that had no contact with humans and therefore had not learned to distrust or fear them. This is what sent him to the Kamchatka peninsula. During the cold war this was a military protected zone, uninhabited, and no civilian was even permitted to visit. Somehow Charlie persuaded the Russian government to allow him to fly in (with a plane he built himself from a kit) and build a small cabin next to a lake, in 1996. Sure enough, the bears began (out of curiosity?) hanging out near the cabin, and often would encourage Charlie to go for walks in the woods with them.

Russell's most profound encounter came in the early 1990s while guiding bear watchers to Canada's only grizzly sanctuary in northwestern British Columbia. One day an animal Russell knew, and had dubbed the Mouse Creek Bear, approached as he was sitting on a moss-covered log. After Russell spoke to the female grizzly in the calmest voice he could muster, she sat down beside him, extended a paw and gently touched his hand. Russell touched the bear's nose and then, without thinking, slipped his fingers inside her mouth and slid them along her grinding teeth.

"She could have had my hand, and the rest of me, for dinner," marvels Russell, "but she did not."

On one memorable occasion in Russia, a mother bear turned up with her two cubs. Legend has it that no animal in nature is as dangerous as a female bear with young cubs. Charlie was cautious. But all the mother wanted was to leave her two cubs with the new babysitter while she went off searching for food. No doubt she had observed how Charlie had behaved with a total of ten baby cubs from zoos (in an experiment to see if they could be habituated back into the wild—they could) and had decided he was a trustworthy babysitter. But his activities and writing drew the anger of hunters, as he explained in an interview in 2009 "because the hunting culture needs to promote an animal as fearful so that people can feel brave about killing it." Unfortunately, through no fault of his, the bears began to trust humans and this allowed the hunters to come in and with no effort, kill them. "They were so easily killed," he lamented, "that's my nightmare image."

Charlie himself died in 2018, and I would not be surprised if grief did not have something to do with his premature death. There were few people who could understand how he could grieve the death of wild bears with such intensity, and no doubt this "emotional isolation" also got to him. He did something nobody had ever previously thought possible, and it opened his heart to a kind of love that most of us can barely perceive. His grief is particularly poignant because it was not shared, just his alone to bear.

Did he love those bears, and feel badly about what happened to them? Of course. Deeply so. Did they love him back? Well, we really can't know, I agree, and love might be too strong a word, but certainly they were well disposed toward him. That is a wonderful achievement. As he put it: "Everyone thought of the bears as being ferocious and aggressive, willing to kill at any moment, but I came to see them as peace-loving animals."*

This also raises a rather delicate question that has been gaining attention only recently: Can we experience such a thing as grief for an animal we do not personally know? I think the answer has to be yes, unless we disregard the many people who experience this (and that is something I believe we should never do—it is the one main lesson I want people to take away from this book: Do not belittle the grief of others). There are many variations here: There are people who watch a video and cry. There are people who attempt to rescue animals from horrendous conditions (chickens, pigs, cows) and when they see how they have been forced to live, they break down in tears. Their compassion and empathy is aroused by seeing (and some-

---

* Katz, Brigit. "Charlie Russell, a Naturalist Who Lived Among Bears, Has Died at 76." Smithsonian.com, Smithsonian Institution, May 14, 2018.

times merely hearing) about the suffering of other animals. I myself have felt the eyes of cows and sheep in trucks when they are being carried to slaughter, fixate on me: I am suddenly aware that they are looking at me. I thought at first they were pleading for me to do something, but now I think it is something even more profound: They are letting me know that they have witnessed me doing nothing. I know this sounds harsh and could well be my own projection. But something about their eyes disturbs me, and I hate passing such trucks. Once I was walking in the South Island of New Zealand past a herd of cows in a field, and they all stopped to stare at me. I walked closer to the fence, and they all came forward and just looked at me with great intensity. I felt ashamed to be there; I don't know why. I felt bad for the fate that awaited them. I felt terrible that I could do nothing to alter that fate. Call that sentimentalism if you will, but more and more people are having this exact same moment in their daily lives, and it is unnerving.

If you enjoy looking for unusual stories on the internet as I do, you will find many examples of extraordinary friendships between humans and other animals. Mostly, it would seem, these are animals who naturally form close relations to others of their kind. If for some reason they cannot achieve this, they will sometimes turn to humans. I was going to add "as substitutes," but maybe I'm wrong. Maybe some animals just choose us because they like us.

When I was about ten and living in the valley in California, I became the "mother" to four young ducks, who had to be prevented from entering the school I walked to every day. They accompanied me, and then amused themselves in the nearby park until school was over, and then we all set off for the walk back to our house with a large garden and a pool (pond to them). I adored them. They were definitely attached to me, but I think mostly because of the famous "imprinting": I was the first living creature they saw when they hatched (I can no longer remember why) and they naturally thought of me as their mother.

But sometimes, a completely wild bird decides to befriend a human for reasons that defy explanation. Such is the case of a wild goose who decided to become best friends with an elderly retired man in a park and would follow him for his daily walk and had to be persuaded not to follow him home as he rode his Vespa. As you can see from this video, sometimes she could not be put off and insisted on flying over his head as he left the park. We do not know how the story ends, but you can bet that this man will be grief-stricken should they be parted, and, as is likely, if he dies before her, she will be the one to mourn.*

At an even further remove are examples of people who simply happen to be living in a situation near to, say, a

---

* https://www.wimp.com/story-of-a-goose-who-befriends-a-retired-man-in-the-park/.

forest or a jungle, and an animal comes to recognize them and then seek out their company. There is no doubt that such people feel honored, singled out, chosen. "This animal recognizes I am special."

Consider this fact: just about every human has the fantasy that he or she would make a good friend to a wild animal, but probably no wild animal has the same fantasy.

And certainly every child has this fantasy (see *The Jungle Book*) of befriending a wild (and usually powerful) animal. Part of the fantasy, I believe, involves the knowledge that it will have to end, and that ending will involve sorrow and mourning. We cannot completely cross the species barrier with a wild animal. It generally does not end well. Even children sense this. Hence, I think, their powerful bonding with dogs and cats. They are, after all, only once removed from their wild cousins and nobody bonds as closely to a cat or dog as a child does.

A word, perhaps, about superstitions: I have a novel explanation. It is that we somehow recognize that there are many things we do not understand. I like to ask audiences what they think people will look back at in fifty or a hundred years, and say, "How could they?" "How could they be so dense?" I am pretty sure that one of those things will be plants. A few years ago we would have laughed at the idea of consciousness in trees (except for a silly but fun 1973 book by Peter Tompkins and Christopher Bird *The Secret Life of Plants*), but today tree awareness is blossoming.

Perhaps we have become more sensitive since the beautiful 1995 BBC series by David Attenborough, *The Private Life of Plants,* which ends with these wise words:

> Ever since we arrived on this planet as a species, we've cut them down, dug them up, burnt them and poisoned them. Today we're doing so on a greater scale than ever [. . .] We destroy plants at our peril. Neither we nor any other animal can survive without them. The time has now come for us to cherish our green inheritance, not to pillage it—or without it, we will surely perish.

And now comes the immensely popular book I referred to earlier, *The Hidden Life of Trees,* which makes clear to the lay reader just how much communication takes place from tree to tree, and how sophisticated their lives actually are.

The reason I bring this up is because I find it very hard to explain why I hate losing plants, but this newfound comprehension of their sensitivity and responsiveness might help. I miss them when they're not there. It might well be that they, too, recognize that I provide them with water and care, and am making their life easier. They certainly make mine easier: I like to be surrounded by green growing things. Actually, everyone does. Even hospitals today recognize that patients do better when they are surrounded by green plants, and can look out on a green landscape from their windows.

When I was young, I "kept" birds. I put that word in quotation marks, because it seems to me appropriate. Birds are really not meant to be kept. They should be free to fly and meet their mates and live their lives as nature intended them to do. That said, there can be no doubt that we form very strong bonds with the birds that we raise, and it would appear that this goes both ways. Since many birds form pair bonds for life (that is they marry with divorce rates nowhere like ours), when they are deprived of a suitable avian mate, they have no choice but to form that bond with us. And they do. I had those bonds with "my" birds when I was young, and recently I was reminded by a remarkable book of just how deep those bonds can go. I am referring to Dr. Lorin Lindner's *Birds of a Feather: A True Story of Hope and the Healing Power of Animals.* Lorin is a psychologist focusing on trauma, especially veterans and PTSD. She founded Serenity Park for parrots and military veterans with trauma issues in the 387-acre Veterans Administration Medical Center grounds in West L.A. That has now moved to The Lockwood Animal Rescue Center for wolves, wolfdogs, coyotes, horses, parrots, and other animals. The parrots were "relinquished" by their former "owners" or they were removed by authorities for neglect and abuse. Lorin, whose sanctuary I have visited several times, has a special gift for getting close to these parrots. I wrote to her and asked her to tell me how their deaths had affected her, and she wrote back as follows, one of the most profound accounts about the suffering felt at the death of parrots that I have read:

Just days before I was going to pick up my two Moluccan cockatoos, Sammy and Mango, to bring them home from where they were temporarily boarding, I received a frantic call from the caretaker. She had found Mango on the ground, bleeding.

With trauma, we often enter a dissociated state. Everything seems surreal. People sometimes describe a sense of time moving slowly or being outside of their bodies and watching their movements from above. I can't recall the drive to pick up Mango. A friend drove, and I held Mango in my arms from the moment we got to the sanctuary until he was at the veterinarian's office. He was struggling to breathe, slowly opening and closing his eyes. There was so much blood I couldn't tell where his wounds were. His eyes were bright and glazed. It was Labor Day weekend, and my avian veterinarian was out of town. I brought Mango to a twenty-four-hour veterinary hospital, and I stayed with him all night.

The veterinarian wrapped up his wounds and stopped the bleeding. He gave him fluids.

Without blood everywhere, Mango looked more like himself.

He slept some, and I leaned close to make sure he was still breathing. I watched his little chest rise and fall. "Please, hold on," I said.

When he woke up, he managed to maintain eye contact. His breath was ragged but steady. He seemed to be feeling better. I ran next door to an all-night restaurant and bought a baked sweet potato, he loved sweet potatoes. He swallowed a few bites. Maybe he'd make it, I thought. He was a tough little guy.

He didn't stay conscious for long. Each time he slept, I silently begged him to wake up again. But by the next morning, he took his last breath. His little body shuddered, and he was gone. The veterinarian on duty said there was just too much trauma.

He had been attacked by a raccoon. Raccoons are smart, they watched the birds and figured out that if they grabbed and shook the wire mesh of an aviary, a bird might fly or fall to the ground. As the bird climbed back up to his perch, the raccoon could reach through the cage wire and grab his foot. The parrots learned to avoid the raccoons by flying straight back to their perch. But Mango couldn't fly. He had to climb up the side of the enclosure.

Maybe he was curious about the raccoons.

Mango was always curious about others. Maybe he even said a final, "Hewwo."

Mango couldn't be gone. How could it be a beautiful, ordinary California day without him here? I still had his blood on me, dried on my shirt. I was shaking, whether from exhaustion or grief I couldn't tell. I loved that bird. He'd made me, and everyone around him, laugh. He was full of affection and compassion and loyalty.

I wish I had taken Mango back to Los Angeles the weekend before. But all of that wishing was in vain. I cried. I slept more than usual. Sometimes I just stared into space, thinking of the things I could have done differently. Sometimes I felt weighed down, detached from the world moving on around me. My little man was gone.

It was more than losing a parrot. I know that now. As a psychologist, I realize that one loss can compound past losses. A snowball gains mass and momentum as it rolls downhill, and so does pain. I knew that some of my grief, which seemed inconsolable, was for others I had lost and not fully mourned. I had tried to bury the pain. Denial can seem so useful at times, but like Bessel van der Kolk, one of the leading researchers in traumatic stress states, "the body keeps the score." Grief always remain in us, somewhere in our bodies and minds.

I can write about this now because I did have the opportunity to work through my losses. I missed my mother. I wished I had had a happier childhood with a mother who wasn't ill. I missed the friends I'd lost through the years. I felt alone. Mango's death spurred me into deep self-reflection that allowed me to forgive myself, the raccoons, and anyone else I'd wanted to blame to make my grief easier in the moment.

I still think about Mango nearly every day, but I would never exchange the pain of losing him with never having known him. His absence on this planet does not mean my love for him is diminished. There is a little place in my heart where sunshine can no longer reach, but that doesn't mean I won't seize every opportunity for love. When I think of Mango, I think of this quote by Kahlil Gibran: "When you are sorrowful look again in your heart, and you shall see that in truth you are weeping for that which has been your delight."

One thing I still felt awful about was that Sammy must have been terrified. It was troubling to think that she had witnessed the attack on Mango. I was glad that she and Mango hadn't formed a mated pair and so she didn't have to mourn as deeply, they were just flockmates. Early on the morning Mango died I drove back to get Sammy and bring her home with me. She was jumpy and agitated, but in a few days she was calmer. She didn't enter a period of deep mourning. As for me, I cried every night for weeks. I kept Sammy close to me for a long time, I felt the comfort of petting those feathers, just like Mango's.

I still grieved for Mango, I missed having that loveable little cockatoo entreating me for petting or his favorite food. Sammy and Mango had been, and still were, my family, and I wanted Sammy near.

She lived with us for seven years.

And then one evening I returned home with my husband, Matt, from a day trip and Sammy was standing on the ground. Not a good sign. Tree dwelling birds rarely spend much time on the ground because there are too many predators. Matt and I looked at each other and without a word wrapped her in a blanket and drove right back down the mountain to our trusted avian veterinarian.

As we drove, I thought about that horrible night when I took Mango, bleeding and dazed, to the all-night veterinarian. This time was different. I had the support of my husband who called our vet to let him know when we would arrive and asked him to prepare the hospital for her. Still, though, I had the same feeling of helplessness, of wishing I could just do something to make her better. It was midnight when we got there. I talked to Sammy in calming tones, but something was very distant about her. She didn't make eye contact. She stared ahead, focusing on nothing.

We sat with her all night, willing her to just stay awake. "Come on, sweetheart, just hold on," I urged.

There was little the veterinarian could do for her.

She closed her eyes. Her breath was shallow. I focused my will on keeping her chest moving. For an instant, Sammy opened her eyes and locked them on mine. She used her beak to grab onto the side of the cage and extended her little foot out. I grasped her toes and she wrapped them around my finger, holding on tight. I willed myself to stand there for as long as she could hold on. It felt like we shared the same pulse. As she slipped away I felt my heart skip a beat, and I had to gasp for my breath. That's when she let go, and I knew she was gone.

Matt was standing right there and wrapped his arms around me. It seemed like it would be too much to bear, and I was grateful to not have to suffer alone this time.

The veterinarian diagnosed lead poisoning. The onset of her illness was sudden, thankfully, but the lead might have been building up in her system for weeks. We fed her a natural diet, we didn't use harsh chemicals near her, and we made sure all her toys were safe. What could have poisoned her? There was a single, old cabinet near the ceiling of her room. Maybe it had lead paint. But Sammy never flew. How did she get up there?

I felt as if I'd failed her. This was Sammy, the one animal, more than any other, who inspired me to do the work I was doing. I had never met another cockatoo like her. I had never invested this much of my life in any one being. We had shared twenty-eight years together. It made me realize why we mourn so much when we lose a loved one; we really do invest our heart and soul in them, and we lose a little piece of ourselves when they are gone.

Except it didn't feel like a little piece at the time. It felt like I lost an enormous part of myself I could never get back.

I could console myself that, at least, she had helped heal more souls than most parrots, or even humans, could hope to. I'll always be grateful that Sammy entered my life. I loved her for nearly thirty years. I still think about all those years ago when she was left alone in a house in escrow in Beverly

Hills and she cried her heart out. That cry got me to come to her rescue but it also rescued me. I still hear the sound echoing through the empty streets of the city. I like to think that she was calling to me. I'd like to think that I answered her call.

One of the most beautiful accounts of the death of a wild animal that has affected many people, especially those on the Pacific Northwest Coast who have fallen in love with orcas (I certainly have) was told to me by the esteemed cetacean researcher, Toni Frohoff:

Objectivity. That's what science demands from you. But when your "subject" is another person—human or orca—the heart can easily engage along with the mind. In research, we are told that never the two shall meet. But we can't deny that both exist in the scientist who is also, despite best efforts to conceal it, is also a person. Rather than trying to pretend our emotions don't exist, we can acknowledge and work around them towards the cultivation of our wholeness as human animals—and as researchers.

Luna was an orca who entered a human community in British Columbia in a most unusual way.*

---

* To learn more about Luna, read: Michael Parfit and Suzanne Chisholm, *The Lost Whale: The True Story of an Orca Named Luna,* New York: St. Martin's Press, 2013.

Luna defied much of what we had come to know of orcas, and that was a lot, considering how individually known each member of the resident orca communities had been. Luna was first seen as a baby in 1999 with his pod in the orca Southern Resident Community. In 2001 he was reported as "missing" and presumed dead, yet later was spotted where no one expected him to be—and shockingly alone—in a somewhat remote fjord called Nootka Sound off Canada's Vancouver Island.

How Luna came to arrive in the Nootka Sound human community remains a mystery as was how, as a "toddler," he survived on his own. His pod wasn't known to enter the fjord and members from these orca groups stay with their mom's natal groups for life. They exhibit a degree of family cohesion rivaling those of even the most tight-knit human cultures.

Upon his arrival. Luna appeared not only eager, but even desperate, for connection and companionship with the people who lived, worked, and played in this fairly remote coastal community. At first, Luna's initiation of playful encounters was met with curiosity, amazement, and delight by the residents. People started to pet him and play games with him with sticks or other objects.

It was evident that Luna was trying to forge relationships with the humans who lived and worked around the water so they might become his "surrogate" pod. Luna was eager to participate with anyone he could find. Akin to a giant, gentle, but occasionally clumsy, aquatic kitten, he tried to play not only with people, but also their boats and dinghies, their outboard motors, and even their fishing gear. This started to be met with frustration by fishermen and other people who were trying to work—or just go about their business—in the midst of this friendly orca's antics. What was a bucket-list blessing out of [a] fairy tale to some felt like a curse for others who feared that Luna was threatening their livelihoods. And some people were even threatening to harm Luna.

Among the people living and working in this seaside community, Nootka Sound was also home to the aboriginal Mowachaht/Muchalaht First Nations tribe. For them, Luna's presence took on a different cultural significance with respect to their spiritual traditions. The Canadian Department of Fisheries and Oceans (DFO), along with the First Nations people, deliberated on and disagreed about what to "do" with Luna. Return him to his pod? Let him stay? Befriend him or ignore him? Agreement couldn't be reached and conflicts ensued.

I was called upon by the Mowachaht/Muchalaht's

Fisheries Department to assist and advise in these deliberations about Luna. He was what scientists referred to as a "solitary, sociable cetacean." Study and protection of these unique individual dolphins and whales who had otherwise been little-studied had become a specialization of my research.* But at the time, it was mostly bottlenose dolphins and beluga whales who were known to be examples of these distinctive cetaceans. Unfortunately, as much as these dolphins and whales had tried to "fit in" and become accepted members of their respective human communities, and regardless of how many admirers they had, there was always at least one person who wanted them to go away—or worse.

I arrived at Nootka Sound with a cadre of esteemed orca and other cetacean specialists I had recommended to be part of the consultation. We agreed that even in the best of circumstances, Luna could not obtain the social bonding he needed from even the most skilled or well-intentioned of humans. Our group made recommendations, petitions were circulated, letters from the public were sent—even from schoolchildren—imploring the DFO to "save Luna." We had left Nootka Sound physically but

---

* Lori Marino and Toni Frohoff, "Toward a New Paradigm of Non-Captive Research on Cetacean Cognition," *PLoS ONE* 6(9), https://doi.org/10.1371/journal.pone.0024121.

stayed deeply connected with news of Luna and our fervent desire to help him. I wrote a proposal with esteemed orca researcher Ken Balcomb to help reunite Luna with his pod, which we submitted to the Canadian DFO. But it sat for months, likely collecting dust, while Luna waited. Alone. Human political agendas prevailed and clashed painfully with the simultaneous beauty and pathos of this innocent young whale who was clearly in need of our aid.

Months later, I was on a research boat on the paradisiacal waters of Hawaii, when my cellphone rang, and a friend told me the news. She said, "I didn't want you to hear it from a reporter or a stranger . . . but Luna is dead." I wasn't surprised but I still felt a punch in my gut. I needed to know if, at the very least, it was quick—and thankfully I was told that it was. I was told that Luna was accidentally killed by proximity to a giant boat propeller. But even if this was not an intentional act, Luna's bloody and untimely death was indicative of the utter and gross incompetence of humans to respond humanely, fairly, and adequately to the great mysteries and opportunities brought to us by other species. I grieved for all that Luna had lost . . . while alive and then upon his early death. Ultimately, I grieved for the greater loss to all of the other species with whom we share this planet while we continued to destroy it.

We have seen that humans grieve for their companion animals of all shapes and sizes and even for wild animals they have forged a relationship with. What about the animals themselves: Do wild animals grieve for one another? I think the answer is an unquestionable yes. When I first published *When Elephants Weep* some twenty-five years ago, this was not widely believed. But now I think it is very much accepted even by conventional animal behaviorists. Can we take this any further? If elephants grieve the death of one of their own, could they possibly grieve the death of a human? Consider the case of Anthony Lawrence, the late author of *The Elephant Whisperer*. When he died in 2012 at sixty-one of a heart attack, on his game reserve, the 5,000-acre Thula Thula in Kwo Zulu in South Africa, two separate herds of elephants, thirty-one in all, made the 112-mile walk to his home where they had not been for a year and a half, and stood there for two days and two nights, without eating, clearly paying homage to their friend, and mourning his passing. I don't think there can be any doubt that this is what they were doing. He had saved their lives years before: He was approached and told that this rogue herd of ten elephants—three females, three young elephants, two bulls, and two babies—was going to be shot unless he agreed to take them on his reserve. He agreed, and it took much patience and calm observation before the elephants would trust him. But eventually they did, and this is how he acquired the name the Elephant Whisperer.

I want to end this chapter with a story about two rats, Kia and Ora. They were named, because they were our rats, pet rats, or rather, family rats. We saved them from a lab in New Zealand and they lived with us as friends. I know, I know. One does not associate rats and friendship, but both our boys, young at the time, were crazy about these rats, and took them everywhere, even, occasionally, to class. We realized just how affectionate rats could be. Sometimes at night we would release them into the house and come morning, they would be snuggled at our feet. They loved to play with us and seemed to take partic-ular pleasure from having their delicate whiskers gently pulled. Domestic rats don't generally live more than two years. Both managed two and a half, and when they died, our entire family mourned them, but our two boys were especially distraught. The boys are now twenty-three and eighteen, and yet they will still say, from time to time, "remember the time that Kia and Ora," and proceed to tell a charming story about one of their antics. So, yes, we grieved for our rats, and Charlie missed his murdered bears, and Val her wombat, and Kim her turkeys, and

Lorin her parrots, and there is nothing to be ashamed of in any of this. You could say grieving makes us human, or you could also say, grieving makes us just another animal.

7

∞

Heartbreak:
Children and the Death of Pets

> It's not our job to toughen our children up to face
> a cruel and heartless world. It's our job to raise
> children who will make the world less cruel and
> heartless.
>
> —L. R. KNOST

I suppose the hard part of explaining the death of a pet to a child is the same as explaining the death of a human, or even death in general. But there is one special difficulty, and that is the affinity children have with the pets in their lives. There is the same innocence. In that sense, they are closer to their dog or cat than they are to an adult human, even a parent. I can remember as a child in Palm Springs when our beloved Welsh corgi was hit by a car and instantly killed—I stared at his lifeless body in total incomprehension. A second before we were running through the desert and now he lay there inert. A second before he was my best friend and now when I called him he did not respond. How was it possible for my universe to be upended in one instant for no discernible reason? I cannot remember what adult words were spoken to me, but they could not have made any difference. My dog was gone. They could not bring him back. My parents were suddenly perceived as powerless. I could not be comforted.

I know that even nonreligious people will tell children that their pet is somewhere else now and will be waiting for them. It seems like kindness. Do children believe it? Religious adults do, and it seems to assuage their grief. I cannot share this belief and so it would be hypocrisy for me to talk of an afterlife for their beloved animals to my children. I can imagine them complaining years later when they realize they were told something that I did not really believe: "But you said I would see Benjy again, and it's not true. How could you lie to me?"

But therein lies the very heart of the dilemma that is death. It is absolute and it is a void, and any attempt to think this through is more or less impossible. Nobody can achieve clarity here. Nobody can wrap their mind around this thought of pure nothingness.

Primo Levi, the great—in my eyes, the greatest— Italian writer about the Holocaust left, in his final book, *The Search for Roots,* an anthology of his favorite texts. One piece is by the Princeton astronomer Kip Thorne, *The Search for Black Holes,* published in *Scientific American*

(December, 1974). Levi introduces the text by saying "Not only are we not the center of the universe, but the universe is not made for human beings; it is hostile, violent, alien . . . we are immeasurably small, weak and alone." Now why, we might ask, would Primo Levi include this as a basic text of his intellectual life? I think I know the answer.

Primo Levi was a newly arrived Jewish prisoner in Auschwitz. At one point, desperately thirsty, he reached for an icicle that was in the windowsill of his dormitory. An SS officer smashed his hand away from the icicle with his rifle. Sometimes it feels to me there are only two kinds of people in the world: those with guns and those without. Levi was stunned, and because he knew some German, he asked innocently *"Warum?"* "Why?" The officer answered in what was to become one of the most famous quotes of the Holocaust *"Hier gibt es kein Warum"* "Here there is no why." Levi never forgot this cruel but accurate response, and applied it later to the whole of the Holocaust. Why? How could it have happened? Or, as the title of a book about the Holocaust by Arno Mayer has it, *Why Did the Heavens Not Darken?* In the end, after many books and much deep thinking, as deep perhaps as it is possible to go, Levi said that there was no answer—or perhaps, as in the black holes of the universe, it is beyond our capacity to understand.

One point that is useless for the child, but sometimes

of immense comfort to the adult: we are so tiny and insignificant in the history of the universe, that even an event of such human horror as the Holocaust, even the murder of six million Jews and millions more non-Jews, fades into oblivion. A billion years from now, less than a second in universe time, it will no longer be known to have happened.

None of this thinking will of course comfort the child who has lost her dog, and it would be cruel to say such things to a grieving child. Indeed, you would not be a very welcome guest at a funeral if you began to give voice to such ideas to those gathered in mourning. "Gathered in mourning." Perhaps this gives us the clue to the best way to handle the death of a pet for a child: memorialize it. A funeral—a gathering of people who knew the animal in question—a burial or a ceremony of some kind to show the child that they are not alone in their grief and that this feeling is a good and noble one that can be shared. Their tears are nothing to be ashamed of. Pet cemeteries are becoming increasingly sophisticated—witness the imaginative ways they remind us of deeper realities. I write about this in my chapter on memorializing the death of our animal companions.

If adults routinely do this for the death of other adults, it is especially important to show children that an animal's death matters as well. I would extend this far beyond dogs and cats. The death of a bird, a pet mouse or rat, a hamster or gerbil or guinea pig, even a goldfish, can have a deep impact and leave a permanent mark upon the child, and it is not for us to dismiss it—and certainly never to mock it by taunting the child ("It was only a goldfish"). On the contrary, we should accord it all the solemnity it occupies in the mind of the child. I particularly like the idea of reading something appropriate—for example a poem about the death of a sparrow, or Elizabeth Bishop's "The Fish" (with the beautiful last lines: "until everything / was rainbow, rainbow, rainbow! / And I let the fish go."); Thomas Hardy's fox terrier, Wessex,* or maybe some of the fine lines from J. R. Ackerley's *My Dog Tulip,*† or Lord Byron on the death of his Newfoundland dog, Boatswain,‡ Virginia Woolf's *Flush: A Biography,* Rudyard Kipling's "Dinah in Heaven," and many more.

There is also a sense, in many children, of being in a

---

* Lady Cynthia Asquith described Wessex as "the most despotic dog guests have ever suffered under." On a visit to Hardy's home in Dorset, with J. M. Barrie, she says "Wessex was especially uninhibited at dinner time, most of which he spent not under, but on, the table, walking about unchecked, and contesting every single forkful of food on its way from my plate to my mouth."

† "Was she happy? I suppose she was happy. She had, after all, fulfilled a dog's most urgent need, she had managed to bestow her heart, and upon steady people whose dull, uneventful lives required the consolation of what she had to give."

‡ Ye, who behold perchance this simple urn,
Pass on—it honours none you wish to mourn.
To mark a friend's remains these stones arise;
I never knew but one—and here he lies.

special relationship with an alien being who *understands* them. Unfortunately, adults often do not get that. I can remember very clearly several times in my early childhood when I had an "exotic pet" (before we knew how wrong this was) that was never meant to be kept, as such turtles were bought at the time in dimestores for a quarter, and of course I had no idea how to care for such an animal, and soon its shell grew soft from lack of calcium, and it died in my hand. I was distraught, and when some of my mother's relatives came to the house and saw me in tears, they found this very funny, and laughed at me, and made fun of me. I clearly remember, though I could not have been more than ten or so, how incomprehensible it was to me that they should react to the death of a loved creature, no matter how insignificant in their eyes, with ridicule. I knew, even at that young age, that this was inappropriate. They were revealing something about themselves that I found abhorrent. The same thing happened when "my" (the quotation marks are there to signify that today we no longer think of owning these animals) goldfish was found floating in his small bowl (once again, today we know that a goldfish should never be alone, and needs far greater enriched space than a small fishbowl) and I was sobbing. This was cause for general amusement. Not everyone reacted to a child's suffering, or the animal suffering, in this way, but too many did, and the effects on children are lasting, as I can testify by simply remembering the pain and sorrow I felt, both at the loss, and at the lack of empathy from adults around me.

I hope that such hard-heartedness, however well-meant, has more or less disappeared, and that it would be a rare parent today who would chastise a child for displaying grief over the death of any animal in the household.

I found this story from the daughter of the writer Janet Gotkin (she and her husband Paul Gotkin wrote the single best book against psychiatry that I have ever read: *Too Much Anger, Too Many Tears*) to be right on target about children and their animals:

It was the winter of 1999 when Sprinkles came home with us. At six weeks, he was fluffy and white and could fit in the palm of my hand. While pregnant with my second child, I had obliged my older child, Mima and searched for a kitten in February. Sprinkles joined our family from the Santa Fe Animal Shelter, where he was born to a feral mother.

Over the years, Sprinkles bound our little family through the birth of my son, Salim, and a divorce from Mima and Salim's father, Ahmed. Sprinkles traveled with us when the kids and I moved to Denver in 2010 and when I began dating my now-husband Jamie.

As the years went by, Sprinkles struggled with

arthritis as we tried a variety of medications to control his pain. At his eighteen-year checkup in January, the vet remarked at how healthy he was and the lushness of his long coat.

By April, Sprinkles's pain was debilitating. He struggled to climb the stairs and would often walk downstairs to eat, stopping halfway to rest, and would be unable to climb back up to the litter box. By the beginning of May, I was carrying him up and down the stairs and cleaning up his messes when he was forced to relieve himself on the living room floor if I didn't bring him to the litter box in time.

After a heartbreaking visit to the vet, where he howled in pain, we made the decision to put him down. Mima, now in Washington State for college, booked a flight home, as did Ahmed from Santa Fe, who was after all once Sprinkles's owner. We made the decision to end Sprinkles's life at home. An appointment was set for a vet service to come to the house.

The day arrived and Jamie took Salim to Home Depot to buy supplies for burial, along with a flower to plant at his gravesite. They began digging the grave before the 5 PM time when the vet would arrive. With all of us surrounding him, we lay Sprinkles on a blanket in the living room, but true to form, Sprinkles led us into the kitchen for a last meal. Pre-diabetic, food was Sprinkles's only comfort those last few weeks.

The vet gave him a sedative and we lay with him and soothed him until he fell asleep. We reminisced about his often ornery personality and his utter devotion to us, his beloved family. Our other cats sat vigil just outside of our human circle as we peacefully said our good-bye, as he drifted off. Once he was gone, Ahmed and Jamie wrapped him in cloth and placed him in the grave. We all worked to replace the dirt and plant the flower in commemoration.

As we stood weeping over the death of our steadfast companion, I marveled at how lucky I was and still am. My adult children, my ex and current husband and my remaining feline companions came together to honor such a profound and important member of our blended family. Sprinkles came to us while our family was expanding and bonded with us through the years as our family evolved and changed.

While death is part of life, we know how sad and devastating it often is. The peacefulness of Sprinkles's death reinforced how essential love and support are. While the departure of dear Sprinkles may always fill me with sadness, it also fills me with gratitude and always with love.

You may believe, like Shirley MacLaine, that death is temporary and you will be reunited with your dog—after all, she famously said "I don't know what it's like not to have what I want," and what she wanted was to see her dog again. She believed they had been together in ancient Egypt in a previous life. If so, you can attempt to convey this to a child. If you don't believe it, pretending you do for the sake of the child is fraught with difficulties as I pointed out above. Please remember that when you are faced with a child grieving for a pet, you are also faced with a child in grief, period, and whatever your thoughts about the animal in question, from dog to goldfish, it is important to recognize the genuineness of the emotions of the child, to honor them by taking them seriously. If even one reader thinks *yes, I hadn't thought of that, what a good idea,* then this book will not have been written in vain.

So the answer to the question if a child can be traumatized by the death of a pet is yes, if the adults treat the death with contempt. Of course you could argue that any adult who would do this would have many other opportunities to traumatize their children, but I would not agree, on the grounds that our culture in general has made grief for pets into a laughing matter for so long that it has seeped into general behavior without having been given much thought. But I agree that in the last years, this has changed for the better in spite of the story I tell (which happened some sixty-five years ago, in the dark ages!).

The worst example of this, I am ashamed to say, happened within my own family. My own mother tried to abandon my cat. It happened like this: My mother, for whatever bizarre reason, was disturbed by the fact that my cat Bootsie slept with me at night and sucked on my pajama top about where his mother's nipple would have been. I was about twelve, so there was no fear I would be smothered. Maybe she was jealous. In any event, she took Bootsie up in the hills behind our house near the Hollywood Observatory and abandoned him there. I only learned about this much later, from my father, and so for me now the worst part is thinking about Bootsie's terror as he tried to find his way home—the false leads, the absolute determination to make it home. And he did return. Learning this also affected my feelings and memories about my mother. He had been left some five miles from our house. For both of us there was the joy of being reunited, and I could hear his ferocious purring as he wrapped himself around me and refused to leave my side, avoiding, for reasons I could not fathom at the time, the presence of my mother. A week or so later,

I learned, she took him farther away and this time he did not return. I knew nothing of her actions, but I was disconsolate. How could my mother have possibly helped me grieve when she was the totally unnecessary cause of that grief? In many ways it was worse than losing my cat to an accidental death, because I can remember the many nights I spent wondering whether he would suddenly reappear and climb into my bed. Of course, had I known the truth, that my mother had abandoned him so far away that he could not find his way home, it would have been even worse, as I would have been devastated at the thought of his hopeless attempts to return, at his confusion and all the dangers he would face, not to mention how horrified I would have been by my mother's callous behavior. I believe my mother took him deep into the Hollywood Hills and he, gentle little creature that he was, would have been easy prey to a coyote, who were then quite common in the greater L.A. area.

Of course, what my mother really wanted her two children to do was to outgrow what she regarded as the childish love of animals and, most particularly, our "ridiculous" display of grief for a "mere animal." My mother was only aping (sorry!) the culture here. The philosopher Kelly Oliver points out, that for some people: "To love animals is to be soft, childlike, or pathological. To admit dependence on animals—particularly emotional and psychological dependence, as pet owners often do—is seen as a type of neurosis. . . . Loving animals as friends and family is seen as quirky at best and at worst, crazy."*

Apart from the thoughtlessness of my mother's action toward my cat when I was young, abandoning him in the hills of Hollywood, she also deprived me of the opportunity to grieve his loss, since I expected him to return, just as he had done once before, at any moment. I waited and waited, and some trust in the world must have left me. The worst thing a parent can do to a child when an animal they know and love dies is to lie to them, saying, for example, they have gone to live on a farm. Because obviously the next question, right after "Why?" would be, "When can we visit?" Eventually the lie will be found out, and the child's natural tendency to grieve will have been sabotaged. In my case, it meant that my mother did not want to hear anything about my cat, obviously because it just reminded her of her guilt (at least I hope she felt guilty). So I was left on my own, which is not fair to do to a child. Every child should be allowed to grieve the death of their animal in their own way, but they should also be made aware that others in the family are grieving as well and want to share the experience with them. It is a delicate time for a child, often their first encounter

---

* "Pet Lovers, Pathologized," *New York Times,* October 30, 2011.

with death, and they should not be left to deal with it on their own.

If we believe that allowing a child to love the family pet with all their heart is good for their soul, which it undoubtedly is, we must be prepared to accompany them into darker realms when that beloved animal leaves them forever. At the very least we can let them know that we are there for them and always will be.

8

∞

Should We Eat Our Friends?

> I have from an early age abjured the use of meat,
> and the time will come when men such as I will
> look upon the murder of animals as they now look
> upon the murder of men.
>
> —LEONARDO DA VINCI

Now that you have nearly finished this book, and you have thought deeply about the grief you felt when your dog, cat, bird, horse, or any other animal who was your friend, died, I want you to consider whether it might not be a good exercise to imagine that you were friends with the face on your plate. Now suppose the chicken you are about to eat for dinner were a bird who lived with you for years and years (after all, chickens can live for twenty-five years or more, like many large birds), would you still be able to stick your fork into it? Could you ask someone down the table, to pass the leg, or the breast, when you had stroked that very same breast when you were in sorrow as a child and your bird seemed to you to be your only friend? I suppose there are a few people who could reply, "no problem," but I suspect they are in the minority. Most of us would be very reluctant to eat a friend. And, while what I have described is a thought experiment, it is not at all implausible, or outlandish. There are many people who bond with chickens, and some who do so with cows, many with pigs, a few with sheep, and likewise with every animal we eat: ducks and goats and of course rabbits and every animal who lives on a farm. This was the topic of a book I wrote called *The Pig Who Sang to the Moon* (or in England, *The Secret World of Farm Animals*). These animals all have personalities, and a life worth living, with friends, family, young, and their mates. They are, just like us, invested in living as long as they can, without harm coming to them or their loved ones. Just imagine the terror of a pig who sees and hears and smells the death of her mother in a slaughterhouse and knows that her turn is coming. She freezes in horror, and to say that nothing is going through her mind at that point is impossible to believe for anyone with a heart. She is immersed in abject fear, just as we would be. And it is so unnecessary. Eating her flesh will hasten our death, and the death of our planet, as is by now well known and well documented by literally hundreds of good articles in peer-reviewed journals.*

---

* A fine example is by George Monbiot, a recent convert to being vegan.

So if something is good for you, good for animals, and good for our planet, it should not be difficult to make the decision to move in that direction. I say "move" because I realize that not everyone can immediately become vegan, or even vegetarian. It generally takes a bit of time: so anything that tends toward either is good: Veganuary, where you go vegan for the month of January, Meatless Mondays, cutting down on any kind of meat, all of these are steps that people take on their way to a plant-based diet. And by plant based, I do not mean *primarily* eating plants, I mean eating *only* plants. But again, if you are getting there, I applaud you. Michael Pollan's famous mantra: "Eat food. Not too much. Mostly plants," could and probably should be rephrased as "Eat food; not too much; *only* plants." When I wrote about this a couple of years ago, people said I was dreaming, but today, more and more people all over the world are taking steps to reduce their intake of animal products. The definition of a vegan is: You do not eat anything that comes from an animal: so, no red meat, no chicken, no fish, no eggs, no dairy, no honey. Also, do not use animal products, such as leather, fur, wool, and silk. I think you can see the logic behind this.

---

https://www.theguardian.com/commentisfree/2018/jun/08/save-planet-meat-dairy-livestock-food-free-range-steak. See also the following article of his with this heading: "Nothing hits the planet as hard as rearing animals. Caring for it means cutting out meat, dairy and eggs," https://www.theguardian.com/commentisfree/2016/aug/09/vegan-corrupt-food-system-meat-dairy.

It is not extreme at all. It is simply being consequential. If you believe that female calves suffer when they are removed from their mother at birth, so that her milk can be diverted to humans, or that it is not a good thing for her male calves to be killed as soon as they are born, because they are of no use on a dairy farm; or if you believe that hens should not be confined in cages where they can barely stand up merely so that we can have her eggs (it was not well known until fairly recently that the male chicks who hatch are not "useful" so they are ground up for pet food as soon as they are born); well then, it stands to reason that you will have to decide not to eat eggs or dairy products for the simple reason that you do not wish to be complicit in the suffering that such products inevitably entail. Eggs and milk in a supermarket look harmless, but their history is dark and involves violence on a scale that is almost impossible to imagine. If you have the stomach, you only need to go on to the internet and you can see actual footage of the conditions under which cows and chickens are raised. Or you can watch a good documentary that goes into more detail, such as *Cowspiracy,* or *What the Health,* or *Forks Over Knives.*

Just as it is unimaginable for us to think of our dogs and cats and parrots as food to be eaten by other humans, so must we make the cognitive and imaginative leap to *all* animals who are sentient, that is, capable of suffering. Humans, everyone now acknowledges, are not the only animals who feel pain, and suffer, and wish to retain their bodily integrity. Just look at how your dog shakes with fear when he or she (mistakenly) believes you are angry and are about to inflict bodily harm on them. They are designed just as we are, to flee any threat to their physical well-being. Death is the ultimate threat.

But the main thing you need to do is very simple: you extrapolate from your love for your dog or cat or bird or even fish, and how much you suffer at their death, and then you try to imagine this on a vast scale, one so very vast that it almost defeats our imagination. But try nonetheless. Something like 3 billion animals (if we include fish) around the world are killed for food every single day. Twenty-five million farm animals are slaughtered every day in the United States. Every year in America more than 9 billion chickens are killed. (I wanted to write "murdered" but I realized how odd that looks when written down, *even though it is actually the truth*.) When we look at world figures for a whole year, we are unable to comprehend the figures: something like 3 trillion fish (empty oceans are just around the corner) and nearly 60 billion other animals are killed by humans for food annually.

Can anyone claim this is "natural," that it is the way things were "meant to be" (whatever that may mean)? Of course not. Whether you believe that humans are meant to eat other animals or not, when we first began as a modern species (some 50,000 years ago) we certainly ate meat, but on a tiny scale, and the killing was surrounded with taboos and rituals and even apologies. (We can see this still today in current Aboriginal societies in Australia where killing a kangaroo is a major event, one not entered into lightly.) Hardly anyone ever feels good about killing an animal. Slaughterhouse workers are notoriously under stress because the work is so awful, so difficult to become accustomed to. It goes against our nature to take *anyone's* life.

As an exercise, when I was writing a book about going vegan (*The Face on Your Plate*) I decided to ask people, as politely as possible, what kept them from going vegetarian or vegan, or put another way, why did they eat meat? Since I had so often been asked why I was vegetarian, I felt it was worth turning the tables. The replies I received interested me. Sometimes I was met with a blank stare, as if to say, what a silly question. I eat meat because everyone eats meat. This was a long time ago. Today, most people know somebody even in their immediate family, who does not eat meat, and everyone has heard about the issues involved, read something or watched something and so the answers now are more complex. So "I eat meat because everyone else eats meat" is slowly becoming obsolete. Other answers have taken its place.

Sometimes people would tell me that humans have *always* eaten animals. That is undoubtedly true. But by the same token we could also say that humans have always had slaves, or treated those perceived as *others* badly, or considered men to be superior to women, or were inherently racist (preferring their own race) and so on. The fact that meat-eating has historically been ubiquitous is not much of an argument for why it should continue.

Mostly, now, I find the answers are generally more personal: "It's easier." True, there is not much one can say in response. Similarly, with "I like the taste." "Even," one might ask, "when you know the suffering involved?" If the answer to that is "yes," again, one cannot object. "I haven't given it that much thought," can make it a bit easier to continue the argument: "Do you think it might be worth thinking about more deeply, given the stakes?" Because that last phrase is bound to intrigue someone who has not given it a lot of thought. "What are the stakes?" might be the next question and that opens up the topic of the environment, of health concerns, and for me, the most important, the lives or rather the deaths of the animals involved.

Some will say: "As long as the animal has had a good life, I don't mind a swift and painless death if a human benefits." But all of these terms are problematic: How are we to define a *good life*? Can we really claim that an animal deprived of everything that makes life worthwhile (friends, partners, children, freedom to roam, and perhaps most important, a normal life span) is leading a good life? Who after all gets to decide that a life is good? (Nobody,

I maintain, has the right to tell anyone that their life is not worth living.) The *swift and painless death* is mostly a form of denial: We really don't want to know what happens at the moment of slaughter, and when we do, the picture is not rosy. Countless videos attest to this. Terror is undoubtedly present; mistakes are made and the death is often slow and extremely painful. And does the human with heart problems, obesity, cancer, and other diseases directly related to eating meat benefit? Doubtful.

Let me become a bit personal here and tell you about my own life in relationship to eating animals. I was born vegetarian: unusual for that time. (I was born in 1941.) My parents were very involved, in the early 1940s, with Hinduism so they decided that my sister Linda and I were never to eat meat. When I went off to Harvard in 1961, I found the effort to remain vegetarian too difficult, and I slowly began to add first tuna fish, then every other animal to my diet. I did not think, then, of the ethical component. It was just easier, and it was what everyone else was doing. I did not give it a lot of thought. Over the years that slowly began to change, and when twenty-five years ago I wrote the book *When Elephants Weep,* about the emotional lives of animals, I came back to my vegetarian roots. For it seemed strange to write about how deeply wild animals experienced the very same emotions we did, and then tuck into them that night for dinner. But I had given absolutely no thought to dairy or eggs. When I met my wife, Leila, in 1994, we were both vegetarian. I had not, at that point, heard much about veganism or a plant-based diet. (Only once, when I fleetingly met Cesar Chavez, and he told me he did not eat eggs or dairy as well as any animals, but he did not explain, and at that time I did not understand why.) It was only when I began to research the emotional world of animals living on farms, that I realized how much suffering was involved in milk and egg production. Then the penny dropped. I could not in all good conscience participate in this suffering. I could only continue to eat animal products if I did not think about where they came from, or what was involved in the production. And this I could not do. Once I knew the truth, I could not unknow it. And so I became vegan. It was a lot easier than I feared, and the feeling of living in consonance with my beliefs was a great relief. It has now been seventeen years, and it is a permanent change. I believe that had I been able to make the connection about my love for the dogs and cats and other animals in my life, I could have reached this point earlier. And just think how many lives I could have saved! PETA calculates that 198 animals are saved each year, for every person who goes vegan. That's pretty impressive. The less demand there is for meat, the fewer animals are killed. If the entire world were to go vegan, *no* animals would be killed for food. Isn't that a goal worth pursuing?

9

∞

Dogs in the Rest of the World

A small dog remembers injustice for 1,000 years.

—CHINESE PROVERB

I have traveled in Bali, in China, in Korea, in Vietnam, in Cambodia, in Thailand, in Laos, in Nepal, and in India. In all those countries I saw something that amazed me: they all had versions of *street dogs*.* This is an interesting term. For one thing, these dogs may be much closer to the original "dog" of evolution than the various breeds we have created, certainly in looks, but they are not "wild" dogs. (And by the way, why is it that the world is so deeply concerned with the Indonesian orangutan, but not with the dogs of Bali, an equally endangered species?) The dingo of

---

* Leila, Manu, and I were recently trekking in Nepal, and were astonished at the number of healthy looking "street" dogs we saw, especially in villages with temples: they would lie in the sun, looking very content and not the least bit undernourished. Some had collars, but appeared to be living, happily, in the streets.

Australia, on the other hand, is a "wild" dog in the sense that you cannot simply walk up to one and expect her tail to wag in joy. Dingos can become tame, but they are not tame by nature. A street dog in India, on the other hand, is always ready to become a family dog. The street dogs I have seen in these countries are more like dogs sitting in cages in a shelter, waiting to be adopted, and hoping for your kindness. The term itself refers primarily to dogs who live on the street, that is, just like *street people* they have no fixed domicile. But unlike some homeless people, street dogs have family, that is, other dogs with whom they form loose packs, not to hunt, as did their ancestors, but just for the sheer pleasure of being with other beings of their kind. It is not the fact that they found friends that amazed me, but the transformation I was able to see, over the years, of the people who encountered these dogs. The dogs may for centuries have been hoping to be adopted into families, but a real transformation has been going on only, I would guess, for about the last twenty years.

I can remember being in Bali and seeing people throw sticks at dogs (called Balinese heritage dogs—because they are not quite like dogs anywhere else; they are genetically unique and have shades of the Australian dingo) whenever they saw them. That was years ago. Starting in 2004, the government allowed the importation of breed dogs and this has been a terrible problem: the Balinese dogs mate with them, and their genetic heritage is immediately destroyed.

It is estimated that the population of indigenous dogs since 2005 has declined by 80 percent because of this interbreeding, and because of people killing dogs they believe have rabies, and finally because of the dog-meat trade, about which more later. When I was last in Bali, in 2015, the situation had changed dramatically: people were adopting "street" dogs and bringing them into their houses, not as guard dogs, but out of compassion and the desire to have a friend living in the house with the family. What brought this change about? Partly it is due to one marvelous organization: BAWA, Bali Animal Welfare Association. This was created in 2007 by an American woman, Janice Girardi who, like me, was appalled to see how the Balinese treated street dogs. Simply adopting as many as she could was not a long-term solution. But she realized that much of the fear of the population came from rabies, and that if she could vaccinate every single dog in Bali, this fear would dissipate. So she set out to take on this heroic feat, and was successful.

When I was visiting Bali, I met a friend from New Zealand, who had adopted one of these unique Balinese dogs, who would sit on the back of his motorcycle, and when he saw anything of interest, would jump off (no matter the speed) and, several hours later, his curiosity sated, he would return to my friend's house in the hills. He could find his way from anywhere in Ubud (the cultural capital of Bali) back to the house, no matter the distance. He was an ambassador for dogs. Everyone who saw him loved him.

Slowly Janice's work was having a visible effect: more and more people wanted one of these dogs, and the dogs were only too happy to become part of a family. I have often wondered how it is that dogs in all these countries are simply waiting for people to wake up to how wonderful it is to have a dog in your home and in your life. In the meantime they do not become feral, or hostile to humans; they just wait patiently for us to wake up.

I make it **sound** like the transformation has been entirely successful. That is, unfortunately, not true. In 2008 the dog population in Bali was estimated to be approximately 600,000. With the outbreak of rabies and the ensuing mass culling, the number dropped to approximately 150,000 dogs. If numbers continue to drop, the Bali dog will be at risk of extinction. Can we grieve the loss of an entire species? Of course we can, and must. Aside from organized culling, hundreds of dogs' lives are lost every week to the dog-meat trade, acts of cruelty, disease, motor vehicle accidents, and basic neglect. The situation is dire and the magnificent animal that is Bali's heritage dog is under threat. In spite of the wonderful work that BAWA does, they nonetheless estimate that 60–70,000 dogs are killed each year for food. So, yes, attitudes are changing, but the Bali dog is still very much an endangered species, not the least reason being that people want to (or do they falsely believe they need to?) eat them.

I often wonder what happens when your culture does not allow you to grieve or in any event, does not encourage it? We are seeing, just about everywhere in the world, a huge cultural shift when it comes to dogs. This is no fad. It is permanent. Of course, there have always been people connected in some way to dogs, after all, they have been with us for at least 30,000 years. So no doubt many people, if not most, would want to grieve the death of their dog. But what happens when the culture (Balinese, Chinese, Korean, or indeed European) does not encourage or did not in the past encourage, what it branded as rank sentimentalism or worse?

Part of the problem is that the Balinese have forgotten some of their own heritage. Bali is part of Indonesia, but whereas the rest of Indonesia is primarily Muslim, Bali is almost entirely Hindu. Being Hindus means that they have, as part of their tradition, an important story about dogs from the revered *Mahabharata* (the *Bhagavad Gita* is a text within the larger epic). This is an enormous book, often called the longest poem ever written, consisting of some 200,000 verses (about two million words) written in Sanskrit somewhere between the fifth century BC, and the first century AD. As a student of Sanskrit both in my undergraduate and graduate degrees, I read much of the text. The story that had the biggest impact on me has to do with a dog. A whole book could easily be written about this episode of the great epic, but in essence it involves the governing warriors of the kingdom, after a great battle that basically kills just about everyone on both sides, becoming completely disillusioned—not just with war, but with the world in general. The Pandava rulers leave for the Himalayas and begin the ascent toward heaven. A stray dog joins them, and even though dogs were considered scavengers, Yudhishthira, the great king, develops an affection for this thin dog and allows him to travel with them. One by one the brothers and their wife (they share one wife) Draupadi, fall behind, that is, they are considered unworthy of the route to heaven. Yudhishthira explains each time why: Draupadi was partial to Arjuna (where she should have loved all her husbands equally); the twins Nakula and Sahadeva were too proud of being handsome; Bhima was proud of his great strength; and Arjuna was vain about his archery skills. All of these moral failings prevent them from reaching heaven. Only the little stray dog and the king continue the journey north; only they remain: the compassionate and mild king, Yudhishthira, who had tried everything to prevent the carnage of the great war over which he feels now complete disillusion, and the faithful dog. They reach the gates of heaven, and there a chariot appears, ready to take the virtuous king into the heavenly realm. He steps up into the chariot, and the dog is right behind him. But the charioteer stops the dog and says that dogs are not allowed in heaven. Yudhishthira then gives a beautiful speech, about how faithful the dog has been to him through the entire long trip, and he will not ascend to heaven if one such as this dog must remain behind. At the end of this noble speech the dog reveals himself to be none other than the god Yama Dharmaraja, lord of death and of justice, and he praises the king for his kindness and empathy. Given how popular this story is, you would think that the Balinese, having been exposed to it as children, would take to heart the lesson about dogs. After all, it does not take the *Mahabharata* to tell us that dogs are faithful. Everyone knows that. The Balinese need merely to be reminded. And this is exactly what the wonderful Bali Animal Welfare Association is doing.

When we turn to cultures where dogs have been routinely seen as food, the situation becomes more complex. Worldwide, something like twenty-five million dogs are killed for food every year (with twenty million killed in China alone, even though it is illegal). I am referring to China, Vietnam, and South Korea, where I was able to see dog meat offered in restaurants, especially in rural settings. (I saw this also in Polynesian Tonga, where dog-eating appears to be traditional and widely accepted.) There has not been a lot of research done on dog-eating habits in these countries, so it is hard to say how far back the "custom" goes, but it would appear to be several thousand years old, at least in China and Korea. Having talked to people in all three of those countries about this issue, it became clear that there was real hesitation to speak about it. The customary explanation has been that people are ashamed once they see how appalled tourists are at seeing dog meat served in a restaurant, and then of course there comes the counter charge: well, you eat pigs, don't you, and pigs are just as intelligent as dogs. True, but I actually don't think this is the reason for the reaction. I think it is inherent to the nature of dogs. Just as the great Indian epic recognized how faithful an animal a dog is, so do people in every culture, including cultures in which dogs are food, recognize their virtues. People might eat them, but I cannot believe that they do not feel a twinge of regret and sorrow for doing so. But perhaps not. A journalist was asking people about this very matter and found an older man who lives in Taizhou, who recalls "waiting for winter so he can select a dog to be dished up, just as one can select a fish to be served in a seafood restaurant."* (Some of us are squeamish about selecting fish, too—I know I could never bear to see this, even as a child: my father ate oysters that were very "fresh," that is, alive, and I was horrified.) If you have had the misfortune of looking at the many photos on the internet of the sad faces of the dogs in cages waiting to be killed, you will know what I mean. They look puzzled, and if anyone approaches their

---

* Lucy Mills, "Dog Meat, to Eat or Not to Eat?" *China Daily*, February 2, 2012, Chinadaily.com.en.

cage with an intent that does not appear aggressive, their tails start hesitantly to wag. They are after all designed to be our companions, not our meal.

It is clear that they are feeling sad, disoriented, and terrified. How can we not imagine their emotional and mental state, when it is so clearly written on their faces? I don't think it is anthropomorphism to recognize the terrible feelings going on inside them. It is simply empathy. Perhaps they are not aware that they are going to be murdered—that concept might not exist for them—but that something awful is about to happen to them is surely the origin of their trembling and awful fear. It is an unbearable sight and an equally unbearable thought. The good news is that in all these societies there are animal advocacy organizations that are stepping up to the plate and attempting to change the culture. Sometimes (as happened recently in Vietnam) they will stop a truck with hundreds of dogs going to slaughter and forcefully release the dogs and take them to a shelter where they will find (or attempt to find) homes for them.

In Korea, there is a special type of dog, called a Nureongi, which has yellow fur, and is regarded pretty much by everyone there as food and medicine, but never as a pet. The origins of this dog are lost: Is it an original Korean dog, like the Australian dingo? Is it simply a "village" dog, or what the Indians call a "pariah" dog? Does it resemble the Balinese native dog? Many countries in Asia have such dogs (probably because the attempt to create separate breeds would come only much later to Asia than to Europe—possibly in the Middle Ages, Europe, too, had such dogs). To some extent these dogs have always been shunned by humans. It is of course impossible for us to know at this distance (somewhere between 15,000 and 40,000 years that dogs have been "with" us) what they were for us originally. Perhaps they were not one thing: for children a sibling; for women a puppy was, just like the children, a helpless being who needed protection and nourishing; for the men, at least for some, the dog may have been a companion, or a guard, or a helper hunting, or, alas, a meal. One thing is for sure: there were no breeds or attempts to fashion dogs into something we found cute or interesting. And that is surely why "village" dogs around the world are similar. Only very recently have we introduced the idea of dogs bred to look the way we want. Perhaps it is wrong to say these dogs were always shunned by humans. After all, this street dog or whatever one decides to call him, must have been the "original" dog that accompanied humans when we were hunter-gatherers. I cannot imagine that the Korean dog is any different in its emotional makeup than any other dog. What it wants is to be part of a human family. The tragedy is that it will never get its wish.

In China, there is the notorious Yulin Dog Meat Festival, held yearly during the summer solstice in Guangxi since 2009. At least 10,000 to 15,000 dogs (and cats) are butchered for their meat and served at the "festival" (what kind of festival is it that allows such blatant cruelty?). Recently there has been enormous pushback both within China, and abroad, since many videos and photos show what are clearly companion dogs with collars around their necks who have obviously been kidnapped from their legitimate homes. The dogs look absolutely petrified; perhaps they are not aware of what is about to happen, but the thought is hard to shake, that they sense something terrible as they search frantically with their eyes for their human friends. You cannot see these images without weeping. "I was in Yulin late last month," wrote Peter Li, an associate professor of East Asian politics at the University of Houston, in a widely shared article published by the *South China Morning Post* in June 2015. "What I saw was a city in preparation for the annual massacre. . . . A slaughterhouse at the city's Dong Kou market had just received a new supply of dogs shipped from Sichuan," he continued. "The unloaded dogs looked emaciated, dehydrated and terrified . . . dogs and cats, many wearing collars, displayed behavior associated with household pets."

As the actor Ricky Gervais said at the time: "Whether you're an atheist or believer, vegan or hunter, you must agree that torturing a dog then skinning it alive is wrong." He is referring to the practice of causing maximum suffering by either beating the dog to death or skinning it alive, as this is believed to improve the flavor of the meat. It is a sickening thought, as much as the thought of the torture that is a routine part of war, from antiquity right through to Abu Ghraib. I wonder if any dog has ever wondered if they made a fundamental mistake in allying themselves with us? No doubt some of these soldiers mourned a loved dog. What prevents them from applying the empathy they felt then to "other" humans?

What I find unbearably sad is the fact that hardly anyone mourns the death of these many dogs. Each and every one has a life story, a history, a biography, that deserves to be known and celebrated in detail. Mourning our pets is our way of acknowledging their individuality, and the way they have enriched our lives. Each and every one of these dogs killed for meat, was a potential home companion. When I read this chapter to a few friends, one of them objected (as I knew would be inevitable at some point) that given all the terrible things happening in China, how can we confine our outrage to dogs and cats? He cited, as an example, the treatment of the Muslim Uighurs in China's Xinjiang province where they make up around 45 percent of the population. In August of 2018, the BBC reported that Gay McDougall, a member of the UN Committee on the Elimination of Racial Discrimination, was concerned by reports that Beijing had "turned the Uighur autonomous region into something that resembles a massive internment camp." Given the scale of this horrendous camp (evidently it contains up to one million people), how can I complain about the killing of 15,000 dogs? Well, in my view, one atrocity does not cancel out another. It is possible to be outraged at *both* the killing of dogs and the treatment of the Uighurs. You might even wonder whether it is possible to see a connection: if you harden your heart to the slaughter of dogs, it is easier to do the same for people who are different, in this case the Uighurs. I cannot imagine a Chinese activist for the dogs saying she is not the least bit concerned for the Uighurs. Not everyone can be involved, all the time, in all the terrible things going on in the world at any given moment. We pick and choose according to our abilities and our interests. I find it hard to wrap my head around either, but I am only competent to write about one, and even that with hesitation because of the limits of my abilities. As long as we are doing something about something!

More and more Vietnamese (and South Koreans and Chinese—I saw it in Cambodia as well), are adopting dogs into their family. Unfortunately, most of these people want a purebred dog (might one say, a Western dog?), a poodle, a German shepherd, a yellow Lab, as if the village dog were a different kind of animal. Of course, they are not. They are dogs, and with any kind of affectionate attention, they will become what they were meant to be:

companion animals who live for us, and in many cases we will come to be people who live for them. It's a win-win proposition.

I read a story online by a Chinese journalist of how when she was a very young girl, her parents gave her a puppy who became, as is almost invariably the case, her very best friend and confidant (dogs never reveal secrets). One day she came home from school to find her dog hanging on a rack in the backyard and being turned into soup. She never got over this trauma. I think I can safely say that nearly any child who saw this would experience lasting effects. Fortunately, times are changing very rapidly, not just in China, but just about everywhere where dogs share their lives with people. It is far more common to see a family in Cambodia or Laos or Korea engaging in a mourning ritual for their beloved dog than sitting down to a feast of dog meat. Maybe dogs were put on earth to make humans more humane, even if it took a bit longer than expected?

10

∞

Rage Against the Dying of the Light:
The Psychology of Grieving
for an Animal

What we have once enjoyed deeply we can never
lose. All that we love deeply becomes a part of us.

—HELEN KELLER

Dogs, just like people, express their feelings at the moment of death in very different ways. Here are some examples I have heard from friends who were present when their dogs passed.

"He fought it tooth and nail every step of the way."
"He looked at me in disbelief, as if to ask: How
   could this be?"
"She whimpered and cast a forlorn look at me."
"She seemed reconciled, but deeply sad."
"He trembled in every inch of his body."
"She merely sighed, as if in relief."

But all these various reactions elicited a single comment from every single person who told me of them: "It broke my heart."

Surely the reason we mourn dogs with such intensity is because we recognize in them a depth of emotion equal to (or as I have already suggested, even surpassing) our own. We love dogs because they love us back. We feel strong emotions for our dogs because they have strong emotions for us. So I believe it is only natural to wonder if they grieve us the way we grieve them, and whether dogs feel equally at sea when "their" human dies. Stories, of course, abound, from Hachikō, the Japanese Akita dog who would wait at the Tokyo train station every evening for nine years after his human companion passed away in 1925,[*] to the latest incarnation in 2014 of Masha, who accompanied his human friend to the Novosibirsk District Hospital Number One in Koltsovo in Siberia, and when his friend did not emerge from the hospital alive, refused to leave the grounds, even as winter set in and the temperatures fell to −20°C and even colder. For one year Masha waited, until finally the hospital staff decided to adopt him as a mascot within the hospital where he now visits the sick and dying to bring them the comfort that only a dog can.[†] The huge difference of course

---

[*] An actual photo of him at the station has recently surfaced, see https://www.thedodo.com/rare-photo-of-loyal-dog-hachiko-1446468544.html.

[†] http://siberiantimes.com/other/others/news/n0030-heartbroken-little-dog-becomes-siberias-own-hachiko/. Also, this was in 2014, not 2019.

is that nobody can explain to the dog what has happened. When it comes to these deep emotional issues, you cannot reason with a dog. Sometimes I have heard a child being comforted with the explanation that at least "her" dog did not have to suffer grief at her death; only the other way around. Elderly people living with cats and dogs do worry that their animals will be left to grieve alone. Maybe they don't go as far as Karl Lagerfeld—who, when he died, left his Birman cat Choupette several hundred million dollars (perhaps forgetting that only the human animal has any interest in money)—but nor do they want their animals to be completely alone. I am not sure there is much that one can do to relieve the grief of a dog or cat.

But can you reason with a human? What, after all, can you say to someone who has just lost their dog or cat? All the clichés that we apply to human death ring equally hollow here. I have never particularly been a fan of Elisabeth Kübler-Ross's five stages of grief: denial, anger, bargaining, depression, and acceptance, for humans, and find it just as problematic when it comes to animals. Normally we do not deny their death, nor are we angry. There are no bargains to be struck. Depression is understandable, if it is simply another word for sadness, and as for acceptance, well, what choice do we have? I fail to see genius in this classification.

Like everything else I have talked about in this book, I feel that the way you mourn, just as the way you celebrated life with your animal companion, is an entirely personal and individual decision. Nobody can prescribe to you what you should do. There is no "correct" way to mourn and everyone will do it differently. Some people may feel that your "acute grief" is exaggerated. Let them think that. They may think you should be over it within weeks. Let them. The truth is that it is not up to them. It is personal to you. One thing that became clear to me, after having trained as a Freudian analyst for ten years, is that there are no experts when it comes to love, and, I might add, nor when it comes to grief.

I think what may complicate things is that so often we are called upon, with dogs and cats especially, to "make the final decision," that is, to euthanize your friend. I have talked about this in an earlier chapter, but it bears repeating that this is not a step to be taken lightly. Even if you feel you had no choice (say the suffering had become unbearable to the animal and there was no prospect of lightening it or of it coming to a natural end), you are bound to feel tremendous guilt. And here I would agree with Kübler-Ross: to deny that guilt would be a mistake. The problem is that with hindsight you may come to feel that it was not inevitable, and that in fact, you did have a choice. This will make the guilt all the heavier to bear. That is why it is so important that you think very carefully before making the decision to end your animal's life. It may help to think: *If I were him or her, would I want*

my life to end now, or would I want everything to be done to
make me comfortable but to give me more time with those
I love?

I talked about the rats to whom both our sons became
extremely attached. One we called Ora (her sister was
Kia, as in Kia ora, Māori for "hello"). She was given the
run of the house and would often find her way to our
bedroom when we could be certain she was safe. That
is, when our cats were otherwise engaged. One day she
went missing and we were all very upset. That evening
Leila and I were reading in bed when we felt a gentle
tug at the sheet: it was Ora, coming to our bed. But no
sooner did we notice than there was a swift movement,
and Meghala, our Bengal cat, was upon her. His claw
sunk into her belly and as soon as we rescued her, we realized she had died instantly, perhaps from fear. We had
a tough decision to face: Did we tell the boys the truth, so
that they would stop waiting for Ora to appear, with the
attendant danger that they would hate Meghala for his
predatory behavior, or did we keep it to ourselves? In the
end, we decided to keep her sad fate from the boys. They
mourned for a long time, but never did it occur to us to
tell them to stop.

Much as I find this difficult to write (I actually don't
know why, except that it is in some sense shocking), I
have to add a postscript to the rat story. Leila, my wife,

was also, just like our sons, completely enamored of Ora. When Ora was killed, she wept more, as she recently confessed to me, than when her own father died! (I guess you can tell she was not fond of the man, still it is a remarkable thing that a grown woman, of enormous emotional maturity and sensitivity, cried longer over the death of a rat than the death of her father, would you not agree?)

When we lived on a beach in Karaka Bay near Auckland, New Zealand, we had two chickens, a rooster and a hen, who were very much part of our animal family. They were especially curious about my writing and would station themselves on my shoulder as I typed on the computer (a book called *Raising the Peaceable Kingdom* as it turned out) and would stay there as long as I worked. They also became fond of walking along the beach with us and Benjy and our four cats. The cats left them alone, because they were more or less the same size. They did not, alas, form any affectionate bonds, something I was hoping would happen. But the danger was that these two chickens had lost all fear of dogs (Benjy of course loved them the way he loved all other creatures he would happen to meet), and we were worried that this would come to a bad end. Sure enough, one day on our walk, a dog came racing along the beach, saw the chickens, and ran after them. They raced away as fast as they could but the dog caught both of them before they could escape into our house, and had I not been right behind them to rescue them, they would surely have been killed. As it was, they were only injured but not severely so. The kids were understandably upset, and we decided that rather than expose them to danger, we should find them a home where they could wander freely in the forest. We found such a home, and the last I heard, they were both parents and grandparents and great-great-great grandparents ad infinitum (chickens, after all, can live for up to twenty years, like many other birds—their short life span in human captivity is solely due to the fact that we do not treat them as companions, but as meals).

The same benign fate awaited Hohepa (Māori for "Joseph") our Dutch giant rabbit, another member of our peaceable kingdom. He, too, became very familiar with us and the rest of our menagerie. He especially bonded with one of our cats, the very laid-back ragdoll, Tamaiti, and we took endless photos of the two of them snuggled up at night to sleep together, with Tamaiti protectively placing one arm over Hohepa's shoulder as they dozed the night away. But he, too, lost all fear of dogs, and he, too, wanted to join us in wandering along our beach, especially in the evening when it was quiet and there were few visitors. The problem was that sooner or later a dog would notice him, and the result would not be pretty. We did not want a repeat of what had happened to our chickens, so we eventually decided, with heavy heart (he was such an affectionate guy) to give him to a bed-and-breakfast called

The Tree House far up north from Auckland. And there he led a charmed life: He would sit on the terrace and greet new guests during the day, and at night, he would wander off into the forest and forage. Until one day, we were informed, he did not return. I have to say that none of us mourned, and so maybe Kübler-Ross is right: denial has a place. As long as we could believe that Hohepa *chose* not to return, we could free ourselves from the burden of grief. We liked to believe that no harm came to him, and he continued his charmed existence, only this time, not in the company of humans.

That is a tough one for us. By us I mean the human species. When we have chosen an animal as our lifelong companion, we like to believe they have done the same. But what if they have not? I think it is somewhat rare for dogs to say *Adios* and head off to a life without the humans they have known for so long (at least I have never heard such a tale). But it happens with cats not infrequently: either they choose to live with someone else, or they choose to live entirely without human company, in short, they go feral. One of our cats in Karaka Bay, Miki, did exactly this, and it was a shock to all of us. He was a much loved and spoiled ginger cat but was almost preternaturally independent. You could not tell him to do anything. One day he disappeared, but not for long. A neighbor, two doors down, told us he had arrived at their house, and would not leave. I brought him back, but the next day he

did the same. And the next. The message was clear: I belong with them, not with you. The male of that household,
let it be told, did not like cats, and so of course Miki decided to sleep on his pillow next to him. He was *removed*
(polite term) every night for a week and finally the man
with the cat phobia gave in. They remained close, but not
forever. Miki left their house just as suddenly and mysteriously as he left ours, and we then discovered he was living some blocks away. Same story, same result. And then
he decided he did not want to live with humans after all,
any humans. He managed to visit enough houses where
he was known to get all the food he wanted, but he lived
in the hills behind the houses, by himself. Odd creature.
But it does make you think: *Are dogs really different? Are
they more like us, or at least most of us, in that they cannot live without companionship?* There are human hermits
(but they are rare I'm sure) and there could be some dogs
that live without human companionship by choice, but if
so, I have not heard of any. Dogs, it seems to me, would
no more choose to live without humans than we would
choose to live without a companion. And as I observed
in the chapter about feral dogs in other societies, they all
seem to share a certain sad look, as if this lifestyle is not
their choice. They look as though they were mourning the
life they wish they had.

The exception I know about are the dogs of Athens. A
friend of mine, Mary Zournazi, a Greek filmmaker, has

made a wonderful documentary, titled *Dogs of Democracy,* and the dogs in that film are definitely not mourning. But that is because they are treated with kindness and with friendship. These street dogs are immensely dignified, and when there are demonstrations against the European Union for the hardships they are imposing on the Greek people, these dogs are at the very forefront of the marches, right alongside the ringleaders. They are respected and acknowledged. They are not hungry, they are not cold, they are a bit like that famous line about parallel nations, going their own way. That, too, would be a nice way to live. When the most prominent of these street dogs passed away, there was a giant funeral, and much of Athens went into mourning.

I am not a great fan of psychology in general (having been a Freudian analyst in what now seems like another life), and it seems to me that more often than not the "wisdom" imparted is more like what one finds on Hallmark cards (a bit harsh, I realize), and in general I prefer weeping on a friend's shoulder than on that of a stranger with a degree. That said, I find it reassuring that almost all psychologists today agree that it is a mistake to put a time limit on grieving, as if anyone who goes beyond what is considered the normal grieving period is neurotic or in some sense ill. Grief in some sense *is* a form of illness and everyone progresses through it at their own pace. So the famous four phases (shock and numbness;

yearning and searching; despair; reorganization and re-
covery) of the psychiatrist and ethologist John Bowlby—
while immensely influential, which preceded the more
famous five stages of Elisabeth Kübler-Ross, are just one
person's theory of how grief should or does proceed, and
you should feel free to ignore them. If you feel sad or depressed, as many people do, there is nothing pathological
about this. And if it continues longer than somebody else
might wish, well, too bad for them. Do not allow your
grief to be pathologized. It is yours. You own it. You can
walk away from it overnight, or you can keep it for the
rest of your life. That is your business, and not that of a
clinical psychologist. Nobody but you really knows how
you felt about your dog or cat, and nobody but you knows
what you are feeling now, and nobody at all has the right
to judge you. No rules, then, no stages, and nobody you
need answer to except yourself. I will make one exception: Remaining silent about loss is never a good idea, especially when you are dealing with the loss of a beloved
animal. We are a storytelling species, after all.

If there is nobody else around, talk to your dog or cat.
They will understand the feelings behind the words, I can
assure you.

11

∞

I Will *Not* Get Another Dog or Cat,
or Will I?

Before you get a dog, you can't quite imagine what
living with one might be like; afterward, you can't
imagine living any other way.

—CAROLINE KNAPP

All of you who have lost a dog are aware of what you
have lost: an uncomplicated physical and emotional intimacy that is hard to have with any other being. Even with
children and spouses we are not continuously stroking
them the way we are with cats and dogs. By uncomplicated I mean that there is rarely any ambiguity: we do not
quarrel and fight and sulk and go off into another room
or ask for our space. A dog is totally fixated on you: if
you are writing, he is lying at your feet, just waiting for
any change of expression to indicate what comes next, for
him, and for you. You are his world. (Cats are different of
course—we will come to them.)

And so it feels that this relationship can never be replaced. How is it possible to have this intense attachment again? Well, it is possible. Not the next day, for sure, but eventually. Why feel ashamed that you crave this? Do not think of it as "replacement," for we know that no human or animal of any kind can be "replicated" or "replaced" (notwithstanding cloning, which I believe will never become popular for that very reason). Of course what you had was unique. But unique situations repeat themselves, only differently.

Rather than say something obvious such as "getting another dog, is a very personal decision and nobody can make it for you or even give you useful advice," I am going out on a limb here and say this: "Yes! Get another dog."

But with one caveat: adopt, don't buy. To many of you, this will be obvious. But to others, it may require a short explanation: as of March 2018, 202 cities in the United States (including Phoenix, Philadelphia, San Francisco, San Diego, and Los Angeles) have completely banned pet stores from selling puppies, and they will only be allowed to continue to sell puppies if they can prove that they are "rescue" puppies. This is because it has become clear that most of the puppies from any pet store come from what are known as "puppy mills" and if the word "mills" resonates with the poet William Blake's "dark Satanic Mills," that is because they are hell.

What is a puppy mill? There are at least 10,000 of them

in the United States alone (and thousands more in other places in the world, including where I live in Australia). There are many videos online of what these breeding facilities are like* and if you watch them, I can assure you that you will never consider buying a dog from a pet store or online again. Meanwhile, in the approximately 14,000 shelters in the United States, about eight million dogs and cats are "surrendered." Of these, some two to four million dogs and cats (22 percent of dogs, and 45 percent of cats) are euthanized every year from shelters, some because they are hyperaggressive (usually with good cause) or very sick, or in most cases, because nobody wants to adopt them. When you think that thirty million families acquire a dog or cat every year, you realize that should they get them from a shelter, the number of euthanized animals could go down to zero. So the place to get a dog is from one of these shelters. More and more shelters have chosen to be no kill (as of this writing, there are at least 200 but the list keeps growing), which means that they will not put any dog or cat to death but will either find a home, or keep the animal indefinitely until they do. The people who work at no-kill shelters are there because of their love of animals. People who run puppy mills, on the other hand, are only in it for the money, and loving

---

* Here is one from the Humane Society of the United States, https://www
.youtube.com/watch?v=ZVyFSTYY7zg.

dogs is not part of their plan. The dogs live in abysmal conditions. The breeding pair are basically in prison for the rest of their lives, in inhumane circumstances that resemble the worst of American prisons: bad food, crowded spaces, no medical care, indifference on the part of the so-called carers to the suffering of the inmates. Everyone who has visited such places agrees: they should not exist, and more and more cities are condemning them outright and banning them totally.

Visiting a shelter is something not to be taken lightly. Because your heartstrings will be plucked, and you will want to adopt *all* the dogs you see. Some of the dogs are sitting quietly, as if they have given up hope that someone will take them in. Others are barking, without cease. I am convinced that one day we will be in a position to translate these barks, and I have no doubt that they will be saying: "I am terrified. I don't know what will happen to me. What is coming? I beg you please, take me home with you. Let me be with you. Let me love again. I cannot live without loving." We can only imagine the terrible thoughts that are racing through their love-starved brains. We have to remember, these dogs have evolved to express love, to give it and to receive it. It goes against their most basic nature to be living in this way. It is pure misery. If you buy a dog from a pet store (and the more responsible pet stores refuse to sell puppies), you are perpetuating this misery. Of course, the numbers, both of shelters, and

cases of euthanasia, would not be so overwhelming if everyone who has a dog or cat agreed to spay and neuter them.
Animals who have this safe and close-to-painless operation
usually recover very quickly and often with a marked im-
provement in their character. They are much more mellow
and less hyper and aggressive. Our cats always spent lots of
time outdoors, and injuries from catfights usually completely
disappear, after they have been spayed or neutered. I know
there are people (especially men) who find the thought of
doing this to a dog as unnatural. Yes, it is. But it definitely
saves lives and I don't think you will find a vet in the country who is opposed to it. Putting a dog on a leash is also
"unnatural" but it is nonetheless essential. So we have to
make some compromises, whatever our philosophy.

There are people who will want a certain type of dog,
and so going to a shelter is harder, as they may not find
the dog they have their heart set on, though often they
will find a dog that becomes just that. In that case, my
first recommendation is that they try to find an organization that specializes in rescuing the type of dog they
want. This used to be rare but is becoming more and
more common. So for example, if you want a greyhound,
there are many groups that save "unwanted" greyhounds
(mostly those who lose races) who would otherwise be
killed, and find homes for them. I got one of my dogs from
Guide Dogs for the Blind, since about 50 percent of the
dogs fail to make the grade (ours slyly refused to perform

and what luck for us that she did). If you do choose to go to a breeder, make certain that you do due diligence: call people who have been there; visit the facilities; insist on seeing how the dogs are kept, and so on. Obviously, some breeders love their dogs and that is why they do it; others are in it for the money. Choose the former, not the latter.

Some of you will want to adopt a puppy rather than an adult dog: this is understandable, because there is no creature on this earth as much fun to be around as a puppy. On the other hand, for this very reason, almost all of the puppies in a shelter will eventually be adopted. And while I find the idea of a no-kill shelter absolutely essential, the reality is that there are still too few of them; the vast majority of shelters eventually have to "dispose" (ghastly word) of the dogs who are not adoptable. They are euthanized. The statistics are not encouraging: A dog has a 50 percent chance of leaving a shelter alive. In some shelters (pounds, rescue centers, SPCAs) the figure is as terrible as one in ten. Older dogs are not so easy to place, and they seem to know it. I have heard this from many shelter workers I spoke to. So adopting an older dog is an act of compassion. Visiting a shelter can be emotionally traumatic simply because all of the dogs are hoping for a home and there is often no reason to choose one over the other, except that we cannot possibly take all of them.

I just received an email from the unstoppable Karen Dawn of DawnWatch (which gives indispensable news about animals and animal advocacy that you often do not find elsewhere). I had read a draft of her book about life with Paula Pitbull, who Karen had believed was pretty typical of pit bulls in that she was a loving and utterly human-friendly pet, but not great with other dogs. That last quality made having her difficult, so, as Karen tells it in the email I just received: "When I felt ready for another dog I walked into the Pound and asked, 'Who has been here the longest who is great with other dogs?' Surprisingly I landed myself with another pit bull, Winky Smalls (he has one eye), who is the opposite of Paula Pitbull in every way, from his indifference to people, to his love of other dogs, to his somewhat aloof personality, to his old old soul and profoundly kind nature." She tells me that Winky Smalls is so good with other dogs that the shelter was using him as their tester dog, to learn about new dogs' personalities, because no matter how much aggression another dog showed him it would never become a fight. Dawn suspects his general indifference and aloofness with human strangers is why he waited unadopted at the no-kill shelter for eight months—he interviewed badly. But he is perfect for her. Every shelter or pound or rescue center has the perfect dog for some lucky person.

Should you get another cat? Of course. But it is not as straightforward as getting another dog, because it is quite possible that you had two cats, and only one of them has died. Well, bringing in another cat is not always simple.

The surviving cat might well resent it, and never get over an initial dislike. In this sense, cats are not like dogs. Dogs are hypersocial and have evolved from a hypersocial species. Cats evolved from the opposite, at least "our" cats: that is, they come from the African wild cat, who is very much a solitary species. Now granted that we don't really know a whole lot about what, precisely, that means, we do know that by and large African wild cats, the ancestors of the domestic cat, avoid one another. (But remember: they have to procreate, and infants stay with their mothers for some time, so they are not entirely without the experience of others of their kind.) So while some cats are very easygoing about being with other cats, some, perhaps even the majority, find the transition to be a difficult one. I have definitely seen feral cats living together in the hundreds, without strife, but having observed them for a longer period, I found that they did not have all that much to do with one another. They were not hostile or fighting, but they seemed almost shut away in themselves. I could be wrong, but if I am right, then it is nothing short of a small miracle (one noted by just about everyone who writes about cats), that cats bond so closely to a completely alien species, namely us. There is no real explanation for why this should be, or why we should be so honored, but it definitely takes place, just about always. It is a rare cat who does not form a close bond with some human being or other, and sometimes with more than one.

But if you have had only one cat, and that cat dies, then of course the only logical thing to do is to take yourself to the pound or the shelter and walk along the cat cages. You will find yourself in a strange world, because what I have seen visiting these places, is that the cats, just like the dogs, seem to know what is in store for them, and they reach their little paws through the bars of the cage, and make the most piteous sounds, begging you to take them. (So even if the cat is fortunate enough to be in a no-kill shelter, I don't think that cats understand the difference, and most must assume this is the end for them unless they can find a family to take them in and love them.) But regardless of what they feel, surely we owe it to them not to leave them to a sad fate. We can see it: Some sit quietly, especially the older cats, somewhat mysteriously aware that their chances are not good. They look resigned. Dignified, but also pathetic. So again, if you have a good heart, consider going against the grain and adopting an older cat. The kittens will all find a home, for sure, but only *you* will take the harder-to-place older cat. She/he will be very grateful to you and will snuggle up to you in bed and make that as yet unexplained sound that is known to cure all kinds of aches and pains, including most of all, heartache. So I urge you to go straight to your nearest neighborhood shelter, and bring home an adorable pussy that will give you years of pleasure and affection. This is such an unlikely historical miracle, considering the "solitary" nature of the beast, that you will derive infinite pleasure just contemplating how rare and wonderful it is.

Let me press my luck and suggest something more: How about getting two pets at the same time? Yes, it will be a bit more work for you in the beginning, but consider the joy you are bringing to the dog or cat: cats, as I have just noted, tend to be solitary, but not if you bring two new ones into your house (maybe even two cats in a shelter who have already been together). They will both be on strange territory, and therefore probably on their best behavior, even with one another. They are more likely to bond immediately with each other than with you and will feel less frightened if they are two. Then think about the fact that most shelters today in the United States will not allow you to adopt a cat unless you agree to keep them indoors. I find this difficult to implement, because cats are so infinitely happier when they can go outdoors. After all, they did not evolve to hang out in your living room. But the American Veterinary Society explains, and just about all veterinarians agree, that cats will live much longer indoors than if they are free to roam outdoors. I have already explained the reason for this: cats who roam are routinely hit by cars (rare is the cat who has car-sense—dogs do better, but even they have to be protected from these terrible beasts). Do not think, though, that you now have no more say in the matter. The American Association of Veterinary Medicine takes the position there are many dangers in allowing cats to roam. There is a delightful article in *The New York Times** by the author David Grimm (*Citizen Canine*) titled: "Yes, you should walk your cat." Now, I have tried and I have failed. But that was with an older cat. It is similar to taking cats for a drive in the car. Most cats hate this. But this is only because they did not do so when they were kittens. I took one of my kittens into the car routinely, and later, it was his favorite activity. He looked like a mini dog with his head out the window, ears flapping in the wind, watching the world go by in delight. I am sure the same is true of getting cats used to walking on a leash and harness. Once they get the hang of it, they will love it, and you will be introduced to a whole new world, or rather, the world as seen by a cat. I thoroughly recommend it. We lived on a beach in New Zealand, and at night our six cats loved nothing more than to go for a long walk in the moonlight. It was pure heaven for me, too.

Now a cat left alone in a house may not be as lonely as a dog in the same situation, but the cat will definitely be lonely, most of her/his time being spent waiting for you. If there is another cat to play with, well, that's a different story; in fact, it's a different world. Why not provide it? As for dogs, I have always been of the opinion that no matter how much fun you are, your dog *always* has more

---

* https://www.nytimes.com/2018/12/05/opinion/walk-cat-leash.html.

fun with another dog. You cannot chase a dog the way another dog can. You cannot wrestle a dog in the same way.
You cannot bite their neck and allow them to bite yours,
and they know this, and will never attempt to play with
you as roughly as they would with another dog. You can
never be everything to your dog (whereas he/she might
become everything to you). As for going away during the
day: well, I need not tell you what a lonely, miserable life
it is for a dog left alone in an apartment all day while
his best friend works far away in a sterile office. He has
only one thought: *When will my friend return? How long
do I have to wait?* And do not believe the old myth that
dogs have no sense of time. Of course they do. Some phi-
losophers have claimed, with absolutely no evidence, that
dogs have no sense of the future. Really? Then how do
you explain their joy when you take their leash in your
hand and say: "Who wants to go for a walk?" They are
anticipating the future pleasure. So left on their own, they
are acutely aware of the passing of time; they are bored
and they are miserable. But if there is another dog in the
house, they have company, and they will be forever grateful. I also highly recommend using pet sitters. Almost invariably the people who do this love being with animals,
and it guarantees them fun and entertainment while you
are gone.

You need, as well, to think about cats left alone (if they
cannot go outdoors). In short, the goal is to bring joy into

the life of an animal who, left alone, will never experience the love this animal has evolved to feel, the love of a beloved companion. This is true for cats as well. A companion, cat or human is an excellent idea. So is spending more "quality" time with your cat. We have made cats sociable; so it is our duty to give them room to express their newly found capacity. You will profit, too.

The advantage of getting another animal into your household is that when you adopt from a shelter, you are helping an animal live a happier life, and you are, should you be grieving the loss of a different animal, being helped by this animal to overcome your grief. You need to concentrate on your new companion, to make his or her life wonderful, because in so doing, you will make your own life wonderful, too!

12

∞

Healing Rituals That
Memorialize Lost Animals

Death leaves a heartache no one can heal, love
leaves a memory no one can steal.

—FROM AN IRISH HEADSTONE

I have never quite understood my reluctance to engage
in rituals. Any kind of rituals. My daughter Simone, now
forty-four, says she wishes her mother (who was born in
1937 in Warsaw) had been more willing to celebrate Jewish holidays, even just Shabbat on Fridays. It would have
given her a greater sense of being Jewish, rather than just
listening to me go on about the Holocaust (which does
indeed form the core of my identity as a Jew). Leila, my
wife today, is thrilled at any excuse for a party, so her
birthday and the birthday of our two boys is always a joyous occasion. But I refuse to celebrate my birthday. (Leila
insists that she will not let me get away with it for my big

eighty coming up—though I will still try to slip through the radar.)

So it's not surprising that I did not do anything external—as opposed to internal—to mark the passing of the many animal friends in my life. I mourned, sometimes very deeply, but I did not mark the passage in any physical way.

Now I wonder about both: maybe Simone was right, and maybe, too, I should have done something concrete when animals I loved passed away.

What could I have done? Which is really just another way of asking you, my reader, what did you do, and did it help?

Recently there was a terrific article in *The New York Times*: "What It Means to Be Loved by a Dog," by Margaret Renkl (June 18, 2018), in which she writes:

As a measure of how deeply dogs are embedded in our own lives, consider what happened when Emma, our fifteen-year-old dachshund, died last month. Three friends brought flowers. One brought chocolate. One brought a homemade strawberry pie. One brought a barbecue supper and an original poem. Two little girls who loved her made candle holders. ("I need some water, some glue, a jar and a *lot* of glitter," the seven-year-old told her father.)

On Facebook, 158 people wrote messages of condolence.

I have, myself, reached out to my readers on Facebook, asking them what way did they find to memorialize the loss of a beloved companion animal. Immediately I started getting interesting replies: I was surprised at how quickly and how definitively people responded. Everyone seemed to agree that it was necessary, imperative actually, to do something special in honor of their friend. Within one hour I had an entire range of options, all of which sounded good to me.

Here are some examples. Teresa McElhannon Rhyne tells me:

We lost a beagle to cancer nearly six years ago. He was a rescue. So, to honor him, shortly after he passed we fostered another beagle in need and found that greatly helped the healing. We wound up adopting that beagle as well, and when she passed just a few months ago, we fostered again. So far we've fostered three dogs in the last few months and adopted one of them (because he reminded me so much of the first one and he was also eight with a heart murmur, so his adoption chances were low). Fostering/adopting another rescue is not a unique way to honor a pet, but it's a very meaningful and helpful way all around.

I agree. Fostering and adopting dogs is a wonderful way to save a dog who would otherwise face a bleak prospect, and it also, as here, is a way of staying in touch with your dog who died.

Dara Lovitz made beautiful tiles in her kitchen with photos of their deceased animal friends. They also had a shelf with cremation urns on them, of all who had passed. Every time she passed these she remembered the animals themselves.

A number of people planted trees in the forest in honor of their dog or cat. I noticed that in Germany there is a movement encouraging people to have simple, rustic memorials on trees in a local forest. Mostly people put up a painting or a photograph of the animal onto a tree trunk. But if you plant a tree, you can watch it grow and each time you return, it will remind you of your friend. Richard Jones told me he planted a hoop pine in the forest, and that pine is now as tall as he is. He reminded me of how important it is to not only be present for the euthanasia at a vet, but to actually hold your animal in your arms as the needle goes in, and look at him or her. Being present is definitely the preferred way to be at this moment.

Here is a fine example from one of my Facebook friends, Grant Menzies:

Jessie was truly a mutt—part border collie, part blue heeler, and lots of parts of lots of other dogs. It was intensely sad when, after eighteen years of bounding and running and ruling the house like the princess she was, Jessie began to fade and fail. She lost her hearing, then her sight. Then dementia came upon her like darkness. We once found her trapped under the dining table, unable to find her way back out from the forest of chair legs. She often spent her days and nights sleeping in front of the hearth, unable to climb the stairs to where we slept and where she had once slept. When we realized that to keep her was to prolong her misery, we gave her roast beef—her favorite—and let her stand on the beach to feel the sea, which she loved. Then we took her to where her vet, the kindest, most compassionate man we know, waited. We held her, and as Dr. Bass gave her the injection, she turned and looked at us with eyes that could suddenly see clearly, and it was a look of such gratitude for what we were doing, that I think this more than her passing most broke our hearts. After we spent time with what had been our girl, Dr. Bass cradled her like a baby and took her away, and we returned home, steeling ourselves to an empty house that matched the emptiness inside us. But a miracle happened. We stepped inside, and both felt that Jessie had never left. All of you who have loved a dog know that the air, the energy, in a house with dogs is different. That air and energy were still there, as if Jessie had followed us down the street from the vet's and was still here, bounding around the rooms. Which brings me to the ritual you asked for. We took the water she had sipped an hour before, and the kibble she had left in her bowl, and placed them on her hearth mat, along with her collar, her leash, her toys. And for a week, we talked as if she had never left, and it was as if she had indeed not given up her tired and painful body. Then, at week's end, we got up that morning and felt a change. "She's gone," I said. And later that afternoon, we had a call from the vet: Jessie's ashes were ready for us to bring home.

I was very touched by this story. It reminded me that people after the death of an intensely loved animal, often have strange experiences: odd dreams, what seem like visitations, visions, sensations they cannot otherwise explain. I am sure that whenever you mention that a beloved animal friend has died, in public, you will not only get sympathy, but also many of these very unusual stories. They are, at the very least, food for thought.

Not all memorials have to occur after your pet has died. I love this story from Jill Hinckley, the sister of one of my old friends. She and her husband honored their dog's life before he had passed away, so he could enjoy the celebration, too. And I loved the dream she had years later, telling her that even death had not dimmed her dog's ability to have fun.

Jill writes:

Our golden retriever, Yeller, lived to be eighteen years old—an almost unheard of age for a dog that big. When he turned eighteen, we threw him a birthday party, to which we invited the whole neighborhood. All the kids and dogs he'd made friends with over the years came to help him celebrate. Although by this time he had trouble standing, he lay on a blanket in the driveway and basked in the attention.

Between his birthday and the time, a few months later, when we had to finally say good-bye, we had decided "the time had come" three or four times, but he would always rally. We were trying to judge the moment when life had become more of a burden for him than a pleasure, but that moment never came.

When one day he could no longer get up off his blanket at all, even to relieve himself, we knew it was time to call the vet in to administer the fatal injection. But although he was clearly embarrassed by the mess he was making, his enthusiasm for life remained undimmed. While we waited for the vet, we ordered a pizza. There was little he had enjoyed more than eating the crusts we would toss him when we got a pizza. This time we ordered an extra large and gave him not only the crusts, but a few whole pieces. He was in seventh heaven!

We had been giving him tramadol for pain, and my husband Ron kept saying "Give him some more tramadol," not because he couldn't bear to see Yeller suffer, but because he hoped it would make him sleep, since Ron couldn't bear to see Yeller still so happy. Was it possible this was still not the time? But we both knew it was, and Yeller knew it was, even if he couldn't help basking in his last few hours of life.

When the vet came, she did in fact give him something to make him sleep before she gave him the fatal injection. This was such a blessing for me, since it allowed me to cradle and comfort him as he happily drifted off, and then leave the room before he actually died.

I continued to dream of him for years afterwards. In one especially vivid series of dreams, he reappeared after I knew he had died, and although I thought he had just somehow been allowed to return briefly, he instead just kept going and going and going, running and playing and swimming and laughing. As though even death couldn't extinguish his *joie de vivre*.

Sometimes whole communities participate in the death of a loved animal. And I am not referring now to a domesticated animal, but to a completely wild crocodile in Far North Queensland in Australia. A large saltwater crocodile who was thought to be a hundred years old, was deliberately shot in March 2019. He was a fixture on a small seaside community south of Cairns. Nearly fifteen feet long, he was named Bismarck, and was renowned for his gentleness. The Aboriginal community there regarded him as "one of us," and claimed that he stayed so close to the homes as a way of protecting the people there against other more aggressive crocodiles. He would sun himself on the banks of the river as people walked by. They loved having him there and organized a communal public service in honor of the "gentle giant" as he was called. The entire community attended.

I would say that the most common form of memorial is a tree. I think that we associate our companion animals with the natural environment. Monique Hanson said: "My ex research beagle has a dedicated tree with a plaque at a local park we used to go to to educate about the horrors of animal testing. I have also buried some of his ashes by his tree."

Most want just to remember. So Shushana Castle wrote:

We buried Lollipop in the front yard, next to the bench we sat on during our mornings having coffee and during our evenings with Lollipop. Seeing her place where she rests gives us joy. We sat around her after she went underground to her resting place and talked about the great times she gave us in our lives. Our neighbors placed flowers on her grave which gave us a lot of happiness.

But others want the animal with them even in their own death: a number of people wrote something similar to what Karen Coyne told me, namely:

I plan to save the ashes from my animal companions through my lifetime and have them buried with me eventually when my time is up. Nothing too interesting, especially because it seems in our society there's not a Custom for losing an animal as there is for a human companion. I felt so much loss when I lost my k9 baby who shared every day of my life for sixteen years and yet there was not one card or gathering or anything. Of course people are sorry for the loss but there is just no standard for what to do. As for my cat, my soulmate, I have his ashes with me. I have a tuft of his fur in a tiny jar. I have a stylized painting of him made by an artist friend hanging. Mostly I reminisce about our time together often.

That should remind us to let people who have lost an animal know that we are aware of their loss and their suffering. We do this routinely with humans, but often forget to do so with animals.

Odd (actually it's not odd considering how deep is the need to believe) how many people reach out to animal communicators in the hopes that they will tell them something about their animal in the afterlife, even when they don't believe in either the afterworld or the possibility of communicating with the dead.

Kate Holmes said:

We buried Dudley, our Old English Sheepdog, in our backyard by the swing. He loved to sit in the sunshine out there. He was memorialized by a beautiful stone and a small metal cross. When he died, a huge piece of my heart went with him. I spoke to a friend who senses animal spirits. She was reassuring and told me that he had made his transition and was safe. Not sure how much I believe in this, but it's nice to hear.

I guess at moments like these, *anything* that says something nice and comforting about the departed animal is received with thanks. Some people, though, believe quite literally in the ability to know what happens to them after death: Christine Scalfo told me that when her dog Rock died, almost ten years ago, it was the worst day of her life.

I contacted an animal communicator about a month after he died. She told me things no one would know. It comforted me as I felt he was still with me, just not in physical form. . . . But the most commemorative thing I did was to make a book of his life. It was very therapeutic for me. Once in a while, I'll look through it (I did last week), and I cry still. I sure miss my boy.

Many people chose to honor their departed companion with tattoos. I suspect that most of them are young. Julie Ward Burges writes: "I have tattoos all over my body remembering all my soulmates. And when I die, it's in my will that my ashes will be mixed with all my animals' ashes. I don't care what is done with us after that—as long as we are all together."

Or, Daniela Castillo:

I got a tattoo of my cat, the love of my life. She went with me through vet school and when I was in Australia studying for my M.S. someone poisoned her and I wasn't able to do anything for my own cat as a veterinarian. I had a huge tattoo done in my back and all that pain I felt in my skin felt like a cleanse of pain from my soul.

Bonnie Richmond says:

I have had, and lost, many four-footeds over the years. I rescue domestic rats and unfortunately their lives are relatively short, two to three years on average. They pack so much love into that short life span. My longest-lived, Faith, made it to 3 years, 4 months, and 24 days. I knew his birthday. The day he passed was the day before my birthday. Like others here, I memorialized him with a tattoo.

Finally, Tyler Zee tells me that when one of her companion animals, Jack, a rabbit she rescued from a meat farm when she was a baby, passed away after years, "I got her tattooed on me," and there is a cool photo showing the rabbit on her arm.

So far, we have not seen any description of human-horse friendships and grieving and memorializing horses. I think the reason may be simply that I have had no experience with horses. I have never lived with a horse, nor was I a horseback rider, perhaps mistakenly believing it was cruel. My thinking was that since the big cats are predators of wild horses, and leap upon their backs to bring them down, it must require tremendous self-control to learn that a human rider on their back is not a predator. I was afraid that the way they learn this is the same way elephants learn: by having their spirit broken. I understand that a domesticated horse is in no way like an elephant. Elephants have been tamed, but they have never been domesticated. So a gentle trainer will not traumatize a horse. And horses clearly feel affection for some humans. And many humans feel great affection for many horses, as illustrated by this remarkable account of grieving for a horse shared by Lisa Marie Pompilio:

> I am reminded of a poem by Lang Leav that begins:
> What was it like to love him? Asked Gratitude.
>
> I met Rebel when I was working at a riding academy. He had come in at the end of the day from the auction and was sick with sadness. He wouldn't eat so I stayed late and hand-fed him all the while saying to myself DO NOT FALL IN LOVE. I already had PonyBoy and I could barely afford him even working six days a week, but something about Rebel worked its way into me. The love of a horse is different from the love of a dog or a cat (I have both). They challenge you and teach you. They are mirrors who show you who you are. Every ugly thing you try to hide from yourself and every beautiful thing that you haven't learned to see on your own. They ask you to learn from these and when you do they give you an extension of them-

selves formed in strength and wings, calms in roaring storms, master of the storms. All of this has to be earned.

It is not to say we got off to a good start. He was angry at the world, I was angry at the world and we constantly headbutted on this. When I look back with clearer eyes I realize how broken we both were. We were both abandoned by people, we mistrusted and we struck out (he half tried to toss me into a tree once). But one day it all just clicked into place and I saw what an amazing horse he was as he let down his guard and let his personality shine through. He was PonyBoy's and my anchor, steady and strong, protective, beautiful, and wild like a summer storm. He always had me as we galloped down beaches and through woods so fast my heart would burst with joy and my anger would melt away. I was safe and I was free. In return I gave him sanctuary and every bit of love I had in me. I brought him out to a farm in New Jersey. He lived his days with PonyBoy and a small herd with a hundred acres of grass to eat and he just had to go out on trails with me, splash in creeks and stand there while I detangled his mane.

I am one of the lucky ones. I had Rebel for just over fifteen years and he lived to the age of thirty-five. At the age of thirty-three he started walking out a bit stiff and the vet diagnosed him with osteo-genic arthritis. I retired him completely from rid-ing, which in itself is a death. The thought of never riding him was heartbreaking but through it a new chapter in our relationship evolved and our last two years together were just as wonderful. The winter before he died was pretty rough and the arthritis had moved from his legs to throughout his body. He started rapidly dropping weight to the point he was almost unrecognizable. He took to laying in the field for long hours at a time and when he would get up he would sometimes stumble. I tried everything from acupuncture to steroids, I was determined to save him. He did rally for a month but I believe it was more for me. Slowly as we ticked off treatment after treatment, I came to terms with the fact that I was not going to save him and that I could only provide him as much love and comfort as I could in those last days. The vet called and told me I had literally tried everything and he was going down-hill again and that it was time to prepare for the end. One of my greatest fears was that he would lay down at night and stumble and break his neck when he got up, and worse still be alive till some-one arrived in the morning. It was also the first time I saw fear in him. He would doze off and if I or another horse walked up on him he would try to jump up. I had him euthanized on July 5, 2017, surrounded by the ones who loved him.

That morning I went out to the field to bring him in. I brought PonyBoy with us. I gave him a bubble bath, made him bran mash with apple sauce and carrots and sat with him as he grazed. I held him till the vet came. They asked me if I wanted to leave him with them but I couldn't let him depart this world in someone else arms. Putting a horse down is not like putting a cat or dog down. They are 1,200-pound animals and they are not going to simply lie down, they are going to fall, and a team of people can do all they can to make that fall as gentle as possible but it's still 1,200 pounds falling. I held his head in my arms and felt him slip away as the vet pushed the sedatives in, his weight falling into my chest. I remember being blinded by tears as the vet said she was going to take his head now as she put the final shot in to help guide him down. When his body hit the ground I shattered. It was like every bit of happiness was ripped from my world; he was gone. After, we brought PonyBoy up to see his body. Horses grieve, too, and these guys had not been separated in fifteen years. PonyBoy needed to see he was gone so that he would not think that his buddy had merely been moved somewhere. As we waited for his body to be picked up and taken to the crematorium, I sat with him and then asked my friend to take a clipping of his hair. To this day, I remain at odds with myself about whether letting him go at that particular time was the right thing, but I know deep down he was suffering and that what I could give him as his best friend was this last kindness and mercy.

I don't think I've ever felt as big a heartache or loss as I did in the days immediately after. It was a physical as well as an emotional pain. I could feel a hole inside of me. I would get a catch in my throat and the tears would come. I felt I could not escape my body, a tomb of grief. The thought of going back to the barn and not seeing him was almost unbearable, but I had PonyBoy and when I saw him I swear he gave me this look that said, "I know you are really not doing well, come over here," and we spent the day quietly, looking out into the field and watching the sunset.

It's a tradition to take the tail hair, and I also took a clip from his mane and forelock. I braided Rebel's tail and it hangs in my bedroom with his bridle and name plate. I had a bracelet made out of a piece of his tail so he could always be with me, and for now his ashes are in my house until I decide where I want to spread them. I don't think I would have made it a day without PonyBoy there to keep me going. A few months later a former coworker acquired a horse whose owner defaulted on her rent. She told me just come ride him, and that he was perfect for me, and after much badgering I went to see him. The only bad thing I could say about this horse was that he wasn't Rebel. After a few months I agreed to take Aragon and he has helped the well of sadness. He makes me laugh and has given me back my wings and at least for a while, out on the trail, I feel a relief from my grief and when we pass Rebel's favorite spots and the sadness creeps in I tell Aragon about Rebel.

But in truth there are moments when I am completely engulfed in grief. It is almost two years since he's gone. I tried filling the hole with anything I could, which only emptied my bank account. There are days when even looking at photos of him are too painful. Many people look at me and say, "But you got this pretty new horse!" as if I should be over it by now. There is no time limit on grief. There is no set date on when you will stop feeling this gaping hole. A few months ago I started grief counseling and I've learned that I should not feel ashamed of my sadness or my anger. I started keeping a book of memories and I take my grief day by day. Sometimes it catches me off guard. A recent day at the barn I had looked out into the field and saw a new bay horse hanging out with PonyBoy and for a moment it looked like Rebel and my heart dropped. All I can do is pick it back up and ride on, and on days when I am not so tender I think about the beautiful life we had together and picture him running free with friends that passed before him, in a big green pasture with no borders. Most of all I think of how he smelled of molasses and earth.

My friend Patty Mark, an amazing animal activist (generally for chickens, but any animal will do, and pity the animal abuser who gets in her sights), wrote to me about a sheep, and I am so happy to be able to include this animal who is so often overlooked:

My beloved Prince died a couple weeks ago and I'm still having trouble coming to terms with it. I moved from my home of thirty-six years so he could have a paddock to roam. Born at the slaughterhouse this dear little lamb was brought to me when two days old and we've shared each other's lives for the past ten years. A kind friend came with an excavator and dug his grave in the front garden of my now animal sanctuary home in the country. My son came and together we laid our much loved and respected friend to rest. Once the ground settles,

I have a huge concrete planter that will mark his grave. This sheep touched the hearts of hundreds of people over his lifetime.

I am glad that I did not only get comments on dogs, but also cats. This is what Julie Govegan told me:

I had two cats. They were both cremated. The first cat was a boy, Puddy, who used to love to stare at water that had spilled on the floor. He was mesmerized by it. This was wonderful because everything else scared him to death. He was a true scaredy cat. I decided to put his ashes in a lake that was calm and peaceful. His sister, Kung Pao Kitty, died a few years after him. She was not afraid of anything. We had taken her to both oceans and she stood in front of them and did not run even when the waves came in, so I put her ashes in the ocean. She was twenty-four when she died.

This reminds me of how each and every cat and each and every dog, and of course I could probably go on to say even each and every fish, is a separate individual, with his or her own characteristics. "Fish," you ask? Yes, see my comments on the tame pufferfish who formed a deep bond with a woman I mentioned earlier in the book.

If there are more comments about dogs and their personalities, it is probably only because we are more in tune with dogs, both of our species being sociable in the extreme. Carolina Meyer says:

Three of my dogs died last year. Two from cancer and one from an autoimmune disease. We buried each of them with their favorite blanket or toy. We held ceremonies at the gravesites and spoke to them telling them what we loved most about them and what we would miss the most. We also said out loud what we thought the funniest or cutest thing they ever did was. Then, after a few days, after each death, we went to animal control and rescued a death row dog. We then continue to share with each other cute videos and pics of the dogs who passed away. We also hold a memorial service on the anniversary of each of their deaths.

I love the idea of rescuing a dog on death row. What a lovely way to pay back the love you got from your own dog. Sharing stories does seem to be the favorite thing to do at the memorial.

Zoe Weil tells me:

We have an area on our property where we've buried our animals. At each grave, we place a large rock that we've found and we etch their names and anything else that seems important on the rock. When we bury them, before we cover their bodies with dirt, we share stories about them. All the funny, memorable things. Their origin story as we know it (since they're always rescued). When we are done, we cover their bodies with dirt and plant bulbs or flowers or a shrub over them. Our son has told us we can never sell this property because all the animals are here.

At first I did not understand why the renowned animal activist, Kim Stallwood told me: "Our beloved dog Shelly is buried secretly somewhere where she loved to go." Why a secret garden I wondered? I do not think of dogs as having secrets (even though they keep our confessions to themselves), and then one of my other Facebook friends, wrote this, and I suddenly got it:

When I was eight and my best friend Goliath vanished when our family went off for the summer, I grabbed a rock and carved his name in it. I brought the rock to the next place we lived and made him a hidden garden. I guess the stories are the hidden gardens in our hearts for each.

That I can understand.

I did not know, until my old friend Jerry Tsagaratos told me, that Peggy Guggenheim's grave is next to the graves of her fourteen Lhaso Apsos at the Venice museum that bears her name.

Some use the opportunity to make a major change in their life, something I think is a wonderful idea. Andrew Begg writes that "When my cat was killed by a car I vowed to give up smoking. I knew then, and still know now that to smoke a cigarette would be to dishonor and disrespect the memory of him. That was thirteen years ago and I haven't wavered."

Gary Loewenthal wrote to me that his cat Mike changed his life as well:

Because of him, I became vegan and an activist for animals—even breaking from my career path to do that exclusively. Before him, I hadn't spent five minutes thinking about animals.

Mike was amazing. He loved food but would interrupt his dinner to come running to me when I came in the door. We took walks each day, with a harness and leash, and I saw the yard in a whole new way. He died five years ago. Every day since, I spend thirty seconds, before I leave the house, in silent thanks to him for opening my eyes, for all he did, for the gift I had of knowing and loving him and being loved by him.

Many of the people who wrote to me on Facebook mentioned that knowing their cats and dogs is what made them animal activists, and often, vegan.

Others did not go that far, but nonetheless did something unusual, as is the case for our old family friend in New Zealand, Rachel Wilson, who is both a midwife and an acupuncturist: "We had a home death—like we had a home birth with our kids—we wanted our dog Kuri to die peacefully at home. We gave her rescue remedy flower essence, cuddled her on her bed, and the vet calmly put her to sleep. The bizarre thing was the dog down the road came and sat at the bottom of our section and howled."

Some of the stories are rather bizarre, but I am very inclined to believe them. Here is an example from the founder of the World Society for the Protection of Animals (WSPA), Joyce D'Silva: "I had brother and sister cats. When the sister died, I buried her in my garden, under a blank garage wall. The next day, I was out there and her brother, Charlie, was staring at this blank wall, like he was 'seeing' something, only there was nothing there, no plant, no butterfly, nothing. But he stayed there motionless, just staring for quite a while."

Another recurring theme seems to be having the ashes combined. Audrey Schwartz Rivers writes: "Dogs and cats were cremated and their remains put in nice wooden or glass urns in our living room in a special area. Per my will, their ashes will be combined with mine and scattered in a special place all together again."

I'm not sure why I find the idea of going to the veterinarian for the final act off-putting, but I do, and I find this approach better: Ginny Kisch Messina tells me she has said good-bye to sixteen cats over the years, and they have all been euthanized at home: "A big tin of cat ashes sits in my office with a little statue of St. Francis watching over it and a montage of photos next to it. They are always memorialized with a donation to a feral cat group I helped established (which was also how many of these cats found their way to me)."

All in all, everyone seemed to agree with what Kelly Carson told me: "Some kind of ceremony is vital to giving your grief somewhere to reside." Well put. It shows them how you care and why this is important, as in this account by Dave Bernazani:

In our little apartment complex in Lafayette, CA, reigned a much-beloved community cat named "Brownie," a handsome Siamese gentleman who had been abandoned by a tenant, and (while we were there) lived a king's life, going from apartment to apartment, eating and sleeping in multiple homes, wherever he pleased. He learned to climb up to our second-story balcony to let himself in and take a nap with our two female cats, who adored him even more than we did. When Brownie was tragically accidentally run over in the parking lot one day (while I was at work), a group of residents buried him in a peaceful, hidden corner of the complex, covering his grave with stones and flowers, even adding some night lights. I built a little bench for my wife and other residents to use when they wanted to sit with him for a while.

He accompanied his comment with a lovely photo of the bench, which had beautiful painted stones in front of it.

Some churches now have an annual Blessing of the Animals, where humans and animals attend. Suzan Porto who started one such service told me that "the event is now in its 11th year and is always very well-attended by congregants and non-congregants. At one point in the service, attendees are asked to speak about their companion animals who have passed. There have been many stories over the eleven years that have brought tears, laughter, inspiration, and lasting memories to the human animals in attendance."

To end I would like to include a very heartfelt blog written by Vegan Annie about her cat, Chimpy boy:

This past Tuesday my dear, feisty, in-your-face Chimpy was laying on our bed where he spent most of his time now. I lay down with him and looked into his eyes and I knew, in that instant, that he had given up. The determination to get better was gone. My heart sank. Wednesday afternoon, after a last ditch effort by the vets to bring him around, I received a call filled with the words no one wants to hear.

There is no hope.

I instructed them to set up a room for euthanasia and told them that I was on my way. When I arrived at the vet, I was ushered immediately into a room that had been set up with a soft bed, a little candle, and the injections that would set my Chimpy free. He was brought into the room in the caring arms of a technician and placed on the little makeshift bed. I was left alone to say my good-byes to the little boy who had brought me so much joy in my life. I picked him up, cradled him in my arms, looked into his eyes, thanked him, told him that I loved him and would always remember. He looked back at me, took a few labored breaths and died in my arms.

I brought Chimpy home in a blanket-filled box which I placed on our bed where he had always loved to sleep. When my husband came home, we buried Chimpy in a spot where we would often find him sitting. I put his collar on him and included a little note in case anyone comes across his grave in the years to come. I want them to know that here

lies a cat who had a funny name and an even fun-
nier tail, a cat who was loved and who loved us in
return, a cat who lived life to the fullest, a being
who mattered.

Doing a good and lasting deed in honor of your loved
animals seems to me the very best thing we can do. A
ritual need not replace, and in fact can contribute to, a
long-lasting commitment to making the world better for
animals.

∞

The Never-ending Grief
of Saying Good-bye

As I was writing this book and talking to people about the death of their dogs or cats, so many have said to me words like these: "I had no idea of the grief I would experience; no sense of the depth of it." Many even said: "I did not grieve like this for the death of my mother or father." "I was completely unprepared for the waves of grief that washed over me." "I could not function at all for weeks after."

An old family friend, Matt Messner, wrote to me about the deep grief he experienced at the death of his dog Rhiannon:

> The hardest death for me was Rhiannon. She was the littlest corgi you can imagine but was a spit-fire with the biggest personality. Super intelligent, everyone loved her as she always commanded the stage as the center of attention and entertained. When I would be walking her, I could sense this

burning presence and in my mind but never aloud, I thought her life would be shortened for all the energy she was expending. She was the brightest of lights, and when she was only nine, she was diagnosed with hemangiosarcoma, a blood cancer that metastasizes quickly and is always quickly fatal. She died sleeping next to me, the one dog we've had that we did not make the end of life decision. I believe it was her decision. The other dogs would not come around her body after her death, as she had already communicated with them that she was moving on. I was so sad, each breath was painful and for several weeks I would audibly sigh and call out her name wherever I was. Sometimes I think people thought they were next to a crazy person as you become oblivious to your surroundings in times of grief. In time, as with the others, they become part of you. Not that they aren't part of you when they are alive but then you are totally in the moment. With their deaths, you become more reflective of how important they were to you.

He added: "I think it's so important for others to know that intense grieving is part of the process of having been given and giving so much love to our furry children. And it's okay for anyone to go through this process and not feel guilty or demeaned because it's not a human."

He is right. I think many people are taken aback at the extent and depth of the grief they feel, because, I think they had, perhaps even unknown to them, been acculturated into the idea that "they are, after all, only animals." This is so ingrained in our society that it is hard not to be contaminated with this false belief.

And perhaps because of this they were unprepared to recognize the depth of their feelings that only became available in death. Odd that one should only know love in death, but I think it does happen.

It is a never-ending source of wonder that we have this intimacy, this utter familiarity, with another life-form. It is and probably will always remain a mystery. We cannot solve it, but we can enjoy it.

But it is this very intimacy that is responsible for breaking our heart. Because in the end, this is what happens with almost all companion animals: their time to leave us comes long before we are ready to let them go. That is why I have so often in this book referred back to children. These animals are surrogate children, and I don't mean that in any negative way. This happens too often: a couple decides not to have children for whatever reason, and they lavish great affection on their cat or dog or bird and people say, sometimes with a knowing smile, that the animal replaces the child. But this is certainly false. All you need to do is think about all the happy families who also include animals, which only increases their happiness. You need no excuse for loving, and nobody has the right to tell you that the animal you choose to shower with affection is not a proper object for it. Of course they are, and in any event, only you get to decide who does and does not receive your affection and love.

This means that only you get to decide how long and how deeply you will mourn the loss of anyone who has been part of your life. This applies to children, a spouse, a relative, any human friend, and any animal friend. Should some "petless" person tell you "enough already" you can safely ignore them. Or better, you can educate them. Or still better: give them a puppy or kitten and watch their life slowly transform.

I have a wonderful friend who is a professor of psychology in London. Animals for him and his brilliant wife were, well, just a nuisance, and certainly not worth intellectual interest. Now, nineteen years later, I receive regular pictures of their puppy and their devotion has no limit. When the time comes to grieve, neither will say it is misplaced.

The phrase "animals make us human" (used as the title of a book by Temple Grandin, and come to think of it, by me, too, in a book with the wildlife photographer Art Wolfe, *Dogs Make Us Human*) is never more true than when we grieve their loss. The reason I say this is because I am convinced that emotions are the very core of our being (hence the importance of emotional intelligence that has become almost a buzzword to replace intellectual skills), and our ability to grieve for the death of a companion animal, or any animal for that matter, even one not personally known to us. It has been pointed out to me that there are people, rare people, who are able to mourn the death of the animals we routinely eat and when they see a truck carrying animals to the slaughterhouse they feel deep grief just as the rest of us do when "our" animal dies—what a wonderful world it would be if these people formed the majority. The animal's death releases emotions in us that we may not even know we had. It is like a gift from them to us, putting us in touch with our deepest nature. People have described to me having felt pure grief when their animal friend died, like some emotion that they did not know was inside them. "It just welled up," one person told me, "and came in wave after wave. I was astonished. Of course I loved my dog, but I never expected to feel this overwhelming grief. It just took over my life. I am so grateful to my friends who did not mock me but expressed only sympathy."

I have wondered, for many years, whether dogs ever know that their end is near. Or is all their emotional energy centered on us? One last lick, one last wag of their tail, in the direction of their best friend in the whole world. Who can help but weep at this moment?

Now after writing this book I am convinced: dogs *do* know that the end is near; they *have* a concept of death; they *are* thinking about it; or better, they are *feeling* it.

It's true that we will never know what precisely they think of it.

I began this book with a dream, I can end it with one. It is a beautiful spring day. I am walking with Benjy through a forest in Berlin when we come across a funeral. We join the procession and arrive at a grave where a coffin is being lowered into the ground. The coffin appears to be open, and so, curious, I step forward to look. Inside is Benjy, and me.

I guess that's how it feels. When Benjy dies, some of me goes with him. As I write these last lines, Benjy is still alive, at fourteen, which is a lot of years for a big golden Lab with a heart problem. His problem: His heart is just too big. It has to be, to contain all that love.

There is a short story by the much-celebrated author Lorrie Moore in her collection *Birds of America* where she writes about how completely shaken her character Aileen was by the death of her cat Bert with whom she had lived for ten years, longer than with her husband. She kept thinking about things he did that amused her or moved her: "Once I was looking for my keys, I said aloud: 'Where're my keys?' and he came running into the room, thinking I'd said, Where's my *kitty*?" Her husband Jack was not sympathetic, and insisted she see a psychiatrist. She agreed with some hesitation, but when she went to see the analyst, she told him: "Look," Aileen said. "Forget Prozac. Forget Freud's abandonment of the seduction theory. Forget Jeffrey Masson." Imagine my surprise at reading this now for the first time, because the author is unexpectedly referring to my investigation of Freud's denial of childhood sexual abuse, which incited much controversy when my book on the subject first came out. Yet I totally agree with Aileen's point that the death of a pet is not the time for engaging in intellectualizing and psychoanalyzing. And certainly not the time to medicate yourself, either with prescription drugs or other substances in an attempt to suppress your feelings.

When you grieve, no matter how deeply, no matter for how long, no matter for whom (dog, cat, bird, horse, sheep, chicken, goldfish, wombat, crocodile) *you* are the only expert of your grief, the only person who is entitled to decide when it is over (if ever) and you do not need professional help, people who think they know your emotions better than you know them yourself. Nobody does. In fact, there are no experts in grief or in love, or any of the important emotions that make us human. All you need is the love and support of your family and friends. If dogs and cats and other animals allow us to feel those deep emotions, then they have succeeded in making us more human. And that is the best thing that can happen to us. So I say to you, all of my readers, celebrate your time with your animals, and when the time comes to say good-bye, do it in your own way for as long as you want, and celebrate their lives and the gifts they have bestowed on you.

Benjy died today, August 1, 2019.

Ilan had to go to Barcelona for six months, and Benjy was in no condition to travel (he could scarcely walk, and could not go up and down stairs). So Leila reached out to her cousin in Bavaria who runs a children's campground in the foothills of the Alps. Ilan drove him down there from Berlin two months ago and stayed while Benjy got used to his new home. He took to it immediately, and, more importantly, everyone there took to him. He quickly became the shoulder that every child cried on (these were kids who had been sent there because of difficulties in their homes) and their night buddy. He *wanted* to walk. But he found it harder and harder. He lay in the sun, and everyone came to visit. Including Leila and Ilan, just a week prior to his passing. When he saw them, he looked uncertain, and a bit confused as if to say: "Who are these people? I seem to know them." And then suddenly he got it and came rushing over, and would not leave their side for the next three days. He licked them nonstop and had a look of bliss on his gentle face. You can see it here in the photo that Ilan took with Benjy looking ultra-relaxed and content, with his face on Ilan's lap, which is his favorite position. He had a kind of a revival, looked alert, full of energy, and even went for a long walk around a lake. He was overjoyed to be with his family again, but clearly, he held no grudge that they had left him. He enjoyed his new home and his new friends. He has that gift of loving wherever he is, as long as he is surrounded by people who enjoy his company. And who could not?

But yesterday Leila's cousin called her and Ilan in Spain to give them the bad news that Benjy was failing rapidly. He could not get up and seemed to be in distress. They were calling the vet as it looked bad. The vet came and said that his lungs and liver were full of water. The vet and Leila's cousin, followed by a large number of Benjy's new friends, carried him out to the meadow, gave him a sleeping pill and when he was snoring peacefully, the vet put him down. He did not feel anything. He is being buried in the meadow overlooking the farm.

Benjy brought so much love to so many people—it was his special gift. He could not stop loving. Everyone and every creature. He loved people and he loved birds and squirrels and even baby mice. There was no sentient being that Benjy was not prepared to love. And they loved him back, for his gentle nature, his kindness, his sympathy, and his compassion, that shone out of him. He had a special charisma that comes to those with a surfeit of love. Manu and I got the news here in Sydney, and we sobbed in each other's arms. But we were both so very happy that just a week ago Leila and Ilan were able to spend that final time with him. It does seem that he waited for them to arrive before letting go into the great unknown. Should there be anything there, I know that they will be blessed to have this creature of pure love.